A Hairst Tae Min' On

Life and times in an Aberdeenshire
village during the post-war years

Brian McEwan

PRESS

Cover photograph:
Vale of Alford in Winter
by Jim Talbot

The Author

Brian McEwan is a Glaswegian but since settling in Kent back in 1967 has been at pains to emphasise when asked which part of Scotland he comes from, that the North East and in particular Aberdeenshire is where he owes his allegiance.

Educated at Aberdeen Grammar School and Inverurie Academy, Brian graduated from Aberdeen University in 1959. After two years teaching in Gourock, he came back up north to teach at Insch and from there went to Nassau, Bahamas from 1964–1967. The remainder of Brian's teaching career was spent in Essex and latterly Croydon.

Brian is married to Ann and their four children have happily increased family numbers over the years by presenting their proud parents with ten lovely grandchildren.

It's now over twenty years since A Hairst Tae Min' On was first conceived as a family memoir but as time went on it became clear that the fifties were a pivotal time which needed recording in their own right. Linked to this and his abiding affection for Alford where he lived between 1948-1959, was an alternative career path in journalism which never quite materialised after he entered the class-room. A Hairst Tae Min' On has finally made up for this omission and the author hopes that his reward in writing it will be the pleasure it brings its readers.

Published in 2011

A catalogue record for this book is available from the British Library

ISBN 978-0-9534534-8-1

Design and typesetting by
Leopard magazine www.leopardmag.co.uk

Printed and bound in Scotland by Robertson of Forfar

Published by Leopard Press
Auld Logie, Pitcaple, Inverurie, Aberdeenshire AB51 5EE

'Remembering is a creative act. Our past is a pile of broken pieces. When we remember, we take these little mosaic pieces and build a new life with them. When we write down our memories...we snatch a bit of life away from death and put it on a level where it can exist longer. In that there's a kind of love'.

– Edgar Reitz, Heimat

FOR RORY

Through frozen rear seat window
of Bluebird bus,
you emerge,
on low slung, motor cycle relic,
eskimo wrapped,
waving bravely at the scholars,
Academy bound;
while you created forests,
and later helped Britannia
rule the waves;
then family man,
but still no rest;
ever the quest to find a context for living.

Perhaps you really were a child
of times long past.

Acknowledgements

To Jim Talbot of Alford Images for his atmospheric cover photograph which captures the tone of Hairst so well. Also for permission to use photographs from the many contributors of archive material to the excellent Alford Images website.

To the *Press & Journal* Aberdeen and in particular to former P&J features writer Norman Harper for permission to use articles and photographs.

To Keith Fenwick of the Great North of Scotland Railway Association for permission to use material from *Rails to Alford* by Dick Jackson.

To James S W Whitemore, The Lord Sempill, for permission to use material from *The Aul' Days* by Sir Ewan Forbes.

To the Local Studies Section of Aberdeen Central Library for their painstaking archive research.

To Lindy Cheyne and Ian Hamilton of Leopard Press for their invaluable support and guidance.

And last but not least to the post war community of Alford who inspired the whole idea in the first place.

Contents

Prologue

Scudding North-East clouds over rain-sodden fields unrolled behind, as a city loon crouched amidst a jumble of household miscellany in the back of the removal van, staring with stomach-churning excitement as Aberdeen slipped away and the lush green farmlands of the shire took over. The road was a ribbon of silver reflecting the fitful bursts of sun and showers on the glistening tarmac.

Skene and Dunecht went past without notice, but gradually the fields gave way to close-packed conifer forest as the van laboured up to Tillyfourie before trundling down the Bog Lowster and through Whitehouse into the bosom of the Howe.

Huddled deep within the family's worldly possessions, Silky was having kittens, but that event had to take second place as the van splashed along Alford's Main Street and shuddered to a final halt outside 'Mayview' on a watery spring day in May 1948.

Aberdeen

N orrie and Alice McEwan hailed from Glasgow where they married in 1935. Two years later, at the tender age of three months, I was transported to the Granite City which, I subsequently realised, must have been quite a culture shock for my folks. After a short sojourn in Holburn Street, the young family landed up at 487 Great Western Road, at the end of a row of tenement buildings next to a large patch of allotments.

Early memories were of a rented ground floor flat with a small hallway off which were a living room with tiny scullery, a lounge which doubled as the master bedroom and a small bedroom just big enough to accommodate a bunk bed and cot in which I slept before being joined at respectable four year intervals by brothers Rory and Ian. In this featureless room, Rory was thrashed for his inveterate bed wetting by Nurse Durward, a wicked home help engaged to look after the two boys while their father was at work and their mother in hospital bringing Ian into the world. A narrow, comfortless bathroom completed what in present day terms would be advertised as a one-bedroomed flat in Aberdeen's West End.

The front of the house faced the road along which trams rattled and swayed between their Mannofield terminus and the city, while the back overlooked an unkempt lawn with a wash house at the side and an Anderson air-raid shelter at the bottom. The flat was accessed from a shiny lobby, its brown linoleum reeking with polish, running from the street door to the back garden. Stairs led from the lobby to two similar flats on the first and second floors.

Mannofield, with the county's cricket ground just up the road, lay right on the city boundary only a short cycle from Cults. From the sleepy little village square of Cults with its white, conservatory-fronted hotel where you could pretend to be a posh guest as you sipped a glass of lemonade on a late summer's day, you hurried down the lane past the little shop with its hunch-backed owner and under the railway bridge to the water meadows of the Dee and the Shakin' Briggie beyond. In late summer the hedgerows were heavy with rose hips which you were paid to pick for the rose hip syrup manufacturers, keeping a few aside for the hairy seeds which were slipped down the back of your friends' necks causing them instant discomfort and irritation.

In the other direction lay the city itself, reached by the trams which dropped me off at Ashley Road Public School, later to evoke memories of slates, screeching slate pencils which must have driven teachers daft, and inkwells and pens with changeable nibs for copper plate script in hand-writing books. Built in classical local council style with surrounding galleries rising above a central hall, akin to a prison structure, the school marked the end of each academic year by requiring its pupils to move to new classrooms in preparation for their step up in age level in August. Stress-induced incontinency marked the passage of the youngest pupils for whom the change in classrooms involved climbing the flights of wide, grey stone stairs from the ground floor up to the galleries above. Clearly traumatised by enforced removal from their familiar surroundings, they recorded their distress through sad little pools on the stairs as they ascended unto the realms of further knowledge and enlightenment. On a happier note, opposite the school was a small grocer's where a penny bought you a selection of delights, from cinnamon sticks which you could light up and smoke, to sticks of liquorice which left you with a satisfying brown Errol Flynn moustache.

At the age of nine I progressed to Aberdeen Grammar School when I was considered responsible enough to cycle to school, negotiating tram lines and granite cobblestones on the way. A rare treat was to get a run to school in Alistair Tosh's father's car. By virtue of the fact that he was a commercial traveller, Mr Tosh was one of the few car owners and stepping out of his car at the school gates was akin to the arrival of royalty. The Grammar with its sparkling granite buildings and sweeping lawns fronted by the statue of its most illustrious former pupil, Lord Byron, was a totally different concept from Ashley Road. 'Freddie' Edwards ran the primary department and J.J. Robertson was the school's celebrated rector. 'Dally' Allardyce, Scotland's scrum half and our boyhood hero, taught in the PE department

Aberdeen Grammar School class photo. The author is on the extreme left, second row.

and Peter Cook, father of Labour politician and ex-Foreign Secretary, Robin Cook, taught science. Slides in the freezing winter, conkers in autumn and marbles in spring and summer made up the scholars' playground activities. At morning interval we queued at the railings to buy hot meat pies delivered by the shopkeeper across the road in a wicker basket, covered by a white linen cloth. Salivating pupils lost no time in sinking their teeth into the delicious pies, releasing a flow of warm gravy to dribble down youthful chins and solidify into patches of grease on ties, shirts and blazers.

Recollections of life in post war Aberdeen were happy, despite dim memories of continuing austerity. Christmas stockings dangling from the mantelpiece, topped with parcels too big for them, bulged mysteriously all the way down to the toes where the mandatory shiny Canadian red apple and its partner, an orange, signalled the end of Santa's bounty for another year. Best Christmas present ever was a second-hand bike propped up against an empty fireplace in a chill living room, glistening in its new coat of paint applied by Norrie during the preceding weeks and hidden at his Woodside office. Leaping on to it I suddenly discovered a whole new Narnia landscape as I pedalled with smoking breath through a freezing dawn into the surrounding countryside.

Train crazy, I played interminably with my Hornby railway layout, fitted by Norrie on to a large plywood base, and watched the real thing through the soot-grimed railings in Union Terrace gardens where 'turntables were built into the ground and made to turn the engines round'. Soon I was getting the *Dandy* and then the *Beano* each week, later graduating to the *Hotspur* and *Wizard,* their serialised stories of 'I Flew with Braddock' and 'Alf Tupper, Tough of the Track' inspiring my outdoor games, while *Oor Wullie* and *The Broons* annuals were regular Christmas supplements.

Beyond the confines of the house, a lump of carbide from the box in the tram depot at Mannofield terminus, spat upon, placed in a golden syrup tin with the lid jammed firmly down and a match applied to a hole driven in the bottom, produced a most satisfying explosion and flying projectile. The Lifeboys and Boys Brigade meetings in Mannofield Church instilled a sense of discipline and organisation which I was happy to relinquish when

I joined the less rigorous and more exciting Boy Scouts with their khaki shirts and Royal Stuart mufflers.

Post war shortages were most apparent in the Co-op grocery and butcher on the corner of Duthie Terrace where basics like sugar, flour and other dried goods were packed alike in brown bags with the product name stencilled in purple lettering on the outside. Carrots, neeps and kale were the staple vegetables, while fruit appeared to be non-existent and confectionery was an unknown word. In the butcher next door, the window display with its stacks of corned beef tins effectively summed up all there was to offer within. Visits to the city's main Co-op department store in Loch Street were a treat for youngsters and we stood transfixed by the cylinders of money zooming around the store on their 'overhead railways'.

On summer holidays an 'open airy' tram got the family from Mannofield to Bridge of Don with a change at Holburn Junction. A walk from the terminus brought us to the mouth of the Don and the invigorating challenge of the chill, grey North Sea. On more ambitious expeditions we boarded a bus at Mealmarket Street for the rolling dunes and endless beaches of Collieston, or caught the Deeside train for a Sunday school jaunt to Torphins.

Holidays away from home were a rarity, though visits to Glasgow, where Grandma McEwan and Uncles Dougie and Ronnie and Auntie Isobel lived, were a real treat. To mark the occasion a taxi conveyed the family all the way from Mannofield to the Joint Station. From the moment the varnished brown corridor coaches with their liveried compartments and comfortable wooden seat toilets drew out of the platform, headed by a snorting Black Five, to their arrival at Buchanan Street, the journey was an adventure beyond comparison. Running alongside the cliffs to Stonehaven, steaming through the farmlands of Grassic Gibbon's Mearns, pausing at Laurencekirk and the vanished stations of Forfar, Alyth and Coupar Angus until a longer stop at Perth where the old inland route ended, you could trace through the porters' cries at each stop, the gradual change from the dour Doric of Aberdeen to the self-confident brashness of broad Glaswegian. As smoke from the engine drifted across the countryside the 'peter dum dick, when did you flit, yesterday morning when I got a kick' rhythm of the coaches crossing the gaps between the rails pervaded throughout.

Sometimes when Norrie and his close friend and banking colleague, 'Mac' Mackintosh drove down to Glasgow in Mac's car for bank trade union meetings, I would sit upright in the back seat, taking in the towns and villages along the A90 and enjoying the fine harmonies of the two men as they went through their repertoire of evocative Scottish melodies, doubtless inspired by recordings of Glasgow's celebrated Orpheus Choir.

Glasgow, soot-grimed sandstone city of multi-coloured trams, contrasted sharply with Aberdeen's uncompromising grey granite and institutional green and cream public transport. Glasgow, the magic stopover on the even rarer holiday to the Isle of Arran, reached by yet another train to Ardrossan and then the altogether new experience of the crossing to Brodick on the Glen Sannox with its gleaming, pulsating engine room open to inspection from the gallery above. Finally, Lennox's bus wheezed its way through Lamlash along the winding, heather-bordered road to Whiting

Bay where the forbidding Grandpa Shanks lived in his little cottage at Kings Cross Point, overlooked by Holy Isle. There, when junk food consisted only of ice cream, lemonade and Smith's crisps, blissful days were spent spinning for mackerel, bathing, beachcombing and roaming wild with our five Shanks 'gypsy' cousins, Tom, James, Stanley, Archie and Ronnie.

At some point, however, Norrie and Alice decided that my cultural development needed addressing and I was enrolled in a weekly class which attempted to inculcate performing skills into its bewildered students. Perhaps this is when I first became aware of things theatrical.

Meanwhile Norrie and Alice had become members of Aberdeen Unity Theatre, a left-wing organisation formed in London and other major British cities during the war years and dedicated to bringing theatre to the masses through the works of socialist playwrights. It was this connection which led to my first acting role as Mamillius in Shakespeare's *A Winter's Tale* which Perth Repertory Theatre was performing in Aberdeen.

Bill Owen, who was to appear as Compo in the long-running TV series Last of the Summer Wine many years later, joined Unity during his RAF stint at Dyce and was a frequent visitor to our Mannofield home. A lasting memory is of balloons and a huge bowl of tinned peaches at a birthday party for his daughter Zandra, held at Mitchell & Muill's tearooms which he hired for the occasion. Such munificence during the lean war years was unheard of and I still wonder how he managed to get his hands on the peaches and balloons.

The following morning I was heartbroken to discover that

my very first balloon, safely stored under the bed, had deflated in the night to a lifeless, crumpled shape.

It was at this time that I experienced method acting at first hand, having been cast by Norrie as one of the starving offspring of a Dorset labourer in Six Men of Dorset, a play written to celebrate the Tolpuddle Martyrs and the birth of trade unionism. It later emerged that, at Norrie's behest, the child actors were starved throughout the day of the performance so that when a pot of boiled potatoes was placed before them on stage, it was emptied in a moment as they greedily crammed the food into their mouths. The play had been entered for a drama festival and the adjudicator singled out the 'totally convincing' performance of the 'starving offspring'.

For Norrie the move to Alford was a demotion, forced upon him by the need to convalesce after eight months in Woodend Hospital recovering from tuberculosis. This in turn had been brought about during the war years by managing the Woodside Branch of Aberdeen Savings Bank on a skeleton staff by day and manning the Bridge of Don anti-aircraft batteries by night. Sadly he didn't do too well there either, when the battery claimed the dubious honour of downing one aircraft over the whole period of the war – and a Dyce Spitfire at that. Fortunately, or perhaps unfortunately for the hapless gunners, the pilot survived and made straight for the battery where he treated the lame excuse, that he 'hadn't shown the recognition signal for the day', with the contempt he undoubtedly felt it deserved. It would be nice to think that he was the pilot who shot down a German bomber which crashed into the town's ice rink on Anderson Drive after it had strafed Great Western Road. The strain of defending the city from imminent invasion from German occupied Norway was not helped by Canadian troops who landed on the beach during a secret night exercise, causing Norrie and his Home Guard compatriots to become helplessly transfixed in a state of shock as their Commonwealth allies cheerfully sprang on to the promenade and brushed them aside.

But all this was as nothing to Glaswegians Norrie and Alice who were yet to discover that even eleven years in Aberdeen were no preparation for life in the Howe.

Transition

Since the autumn of 1947 Norrie had been running the bank's diminutive Alford branch attached to the cottage in Main Street. A city bank manager's habits die hard, yet it must have taken some considerable strength of character to maintain the standards imbued since Glasgow days as, immaculately turned out in patent leather black shoes, black suit and tie, hat and rolled umbrella, he made his way down Main Street past the two major Clydesdale and Commercial banks to his modest office built into the corner of Mayview cottage. Later in life he was to remark wryly that while he didn't gain any more customers, he hadn't driven any away.

Added to this was the weekly commute back home to the city every weekend. The dreary one-and-a-half-hour 25-mile bus journey in the 'bleak mid winter' was followed by a draughty tram ride out to Mannofield where the initial delight of the weekly family reunion was dimmed by the contemplation of the depressing return journey on Sunday evening. This was shared with Miss Gray ('the Grayser') who was returning from a weekend spent at the family home in Udny to her teaching post at Alford School. One could be forgiven for expecting the monotony of the journey to have been broken by light-hearted conversation between the bank manager and the young Aberdeen University graduate with whom he shared lodgings in Alford. *Au contraire.* Norrie was saddened to discover that having been exposed to the realms of academia and having acquired an M.A. degree for her pains, Miss Gray had 'arrived' as they say, and saw no reason to progress her own learning and intellect beyond that required for the exigencies of teaching in a country school. There may however have been on Norrie's part, a hint of sour grapes from someone who had been denied a higher education through recurrent childhood illness. Be that as it may, Miss Gray left the bus at Kemnay where she was met by her sweetheart Johnny Comfort for the remainder of the drive to Alford where he worked for the family plumbing firm. Whether Norrie or Miss Gray was the more relieved is still open to debate. In the meantime the bus trundled on for a further twelve miles or so before wheezing to a stop in Alford's darkened and deserted Main Street. A short walk up Greystone Road took Norrie to the lodgings run by the voluble Mrs Grassick who was to become his family's invaluable local contact and interpreter.

Mrs Grassick's bungalow stood towards the end of Greystone Road, opposite the short lane leading to the school. A little further up, just beyond the Pleasure Park and 'Meldie's', the local chipper, the road gave way to open country. Mrs Grassick was a widow, sharing her home with her only son Willie, Norrie and

Miss Gray. The remaining occupants, slavishly responsive to her strident voice, were a cat which she referred to appropriately enough as 'Cat', and an intelligent black Scotty and Pekinese cross, no doubt offspring of its father's illegal encounter with a canine asylum seeker from Peking.

Mrs Grassick presided over an immaculate household in which featured prominently a highly polished and magnificent array of silverware trophies won over the years by her husband, a renowned cattle breeder. In the kitchen, however, a farming background dictated her response to rationing, then still a fact of life. Blowing her whole week's ration in one, she would create a huge pot of thick and nutritious broth which, when the stock ran out, provided cold beef and neeps over the remainder of the week.

At 11 years old, Willie Grassick was the fastest runner in the village. This athleticism had been inherited from his father, also a great runner in his time. Though good natured, Willie was a very nervous boy and particularly scared in the dark. With a limited choice of activities in the village during the winter of 1947, he didn't have too much difficulty in persuading Norrie to accompany him to the Glen Cinema, an itinerant one man outfit which presented once weekly picters of dubious quality in the village hall. Clearly Willie thought that Norrie's presence on the short walk back in pitch darkness would deter any potential Alford mugger. Possibly as a result of this earlier 'minder' relationship, Willie and I became firm friends. A keen follower of wrestling, Willie set up his own ring in the garage at the side of the house. In theory, the bicycle tyre inner tubes

The author with Willie Grassick

attaching the ropes to each corner of the garage would absorb the impact of adolescent bodies and catapult them back into the ring. In this they signally failed and the wrestling bouts were frequently brought to a premature conclusion by collision with the garage walls. Many years later Willie and I met up in Aberdeen's Castlegate Bar and reminisced on our Alford days. We were never to meet again. Sadly, after a career in the Scots Guards and Grampian Police, Willie died suddenly of heart failure in his early fifties.

Transition

The impending move to Alford caused Norrie and Alice to address considerations unknown in Mannofield. Mayview's front, back and side doors with their direct exposure to the elements, for instance, while raising serious concerns for the city dwellers, would have provoked derisive laughter from the local populace. Add to this a tailor's workshop in the back of the house, two substantial front rooms and three upstairs bedrooms and you were left with only one heated living room which, in winter, effectively served as Scott's survival tent in the midst of an Arctic exterior where condensation created fantastical foliage patterns inside the frozen windows.

In the cold early spring of 1948 Norrie introduced Alice to Mrs Grassick who promptly christened her 'Lady Betty'. The couple took their first walk through Haughton woods where they found Haughton House and its grounds, derelict and in a state of decay. As they made their way through the leafless woods of silver birch and giant beech they sadly contemplated the inevitable move from city to country. The prospect of leaving behind established friendships, arriving in a village of strangers and having to adjust to the alien culture of the country after having been born, bred, grown up, lived and worked in a city, was indeed a formidable one.

Arrival

We arrived under lowering skies on mart day. The village came alive as the beasts splattered their way down Main Street, swinging right by the squat Station Garage, up the lane and into the mart itself. First out of the van was Rory's bike which quickly found its way under the wheels of the local slater's car. Happily, accident prone Rory was not part of the mangled wreckage, though the incident probably established the family there and then as 'thae banker feels frae Aiberdeen'.

But for a small area of 'chuckies', enclosed by a low wall topped with ludicrously heavy iron railings which Churchill had obviously missed, the front door of Mayview opened directly on to Main Street. On either side of the door, bay windows projected from the two front rooms. Above, dormer windows thrust out from the slate roof, marking the three bedrooms. Underneath the end bedroom crouched the little branch office, its frosted plate glass window with the Aberdeen Savings Bank logo designed to encourage thrift amongst the local populace and, in so doing, sustain the demanding occupants of the house itself. At the rear of the house, the roof sloped down sharply and then almost levelled off so that you could touch the gutter over the low back door. Jutting scornfully out from the upper part of the roof was a later conversion in total disproportion to the unpretentious slates from whence it had sprung. This strange appendage, testament to either the creative skills or sense of humour of a local builder, housed a rather grand bathroom. Two other doors at opposite sides of the house gave access to the kitchen and rear of the bank respectively.

The interior was a delight. Stairs with handsome banisters (subsequently discovered to have come from the Forbes estate of Newe up in Strathdon) curved up from the hallway, branching off on one side to the bathroom and on the other to a landing which gave access to a box room and the three bedrooms. Below, two spacious front rooms, a generous kitchen, scullery and a former tailor's workshop completed the palatial accommodation. Entry to the small and somewhat spartan office itself could be made through either a 'secret' cupboard in a corner of the adjoining front room or from the workshop at the back of the house.

Mayview was a veritable mansion. Moving from the one-bedroomed ground floor flat of a three-storey Mannofield tenement to this, was sheer ecstasy. And upstairs; an airy, bright yellow wood panelled bathroom with a view over the fields beyond; three bedrooms – one exclusively for me; a strange old workshop; sheds and outhouses; a garden with trees and bushes which would later hang heavy with blackcurrants, red currants

Mayview then

Mayview today

and raspberries; bulging strawberries and explosions of multi-coloured lupins. Backing on to the mart, it presented a grandstand view of the cattle and sheep as they were herded into their pens every Tuesday. Beyond the mart rose a descending belt of firs known locally as The Beltie, while the slope itself provided excellent sledging during the North-East winters which never failed to deliver snow in abundance.

The Beltie

In the 17th April 1947 edition of the long extinct *Aberdeen Weekly Journal,* popular journalist Robert Smith, better known by his pen-name Robin Adair, chose to focus on Alford in his 'Mirror of the North' series. Britain had just begun to emerge from one of the worst winters in living memory and his feature momentarily and beautifully, almost in Grassic Gibbon style, captures the spirit of the vale and its people as they embrace spring and renew the seasonal cycle after weeks of privation.

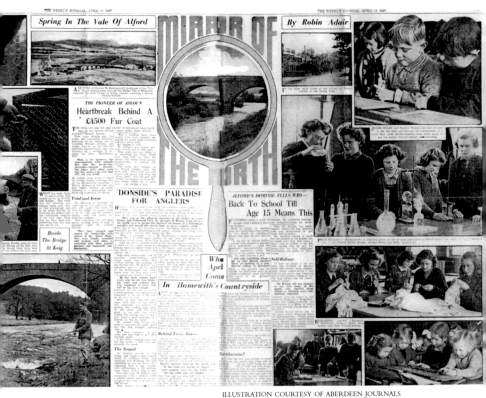

ILLUSTRATION COURTESY OF ABERDEEN JOURNALS

66 Away on the skyline the liquid blue smoke from the burning heather clung lazily to the soft slopes of Calivar. There was a flash of pure gold as a panicking yellow-hammer broke from the bushes. And in the distance the muffled drone of a farm tractor made real the spreading stillness of the countryside.

But this was a pregnant tranquility – an expectancy – as the countryside with its infinite capacity for waiting, paused a while, husbanding its forces, ready to burst into colour, into song and music with the Spring that was surely in the air.

And where better to wait than here in the lovely Vale of Alford where quietly flows the Don… where nature's genius in subtle restraint has made beauty from the most hum-drum of the rural scene.

Down by the water's edge at Montgarrie the fishermen found time

Arrival

to pause and even Farmer Murray – hard pressed and behind times like the rest of his neighbours – whistled a lilt as he threw fresh feed to his livestock and opined that all would yet be well.

Forty years previously, Hamewith – his distinguished relative – had remembered such a time in Alford's Vale and had written:

> There's burstin' buds on the larick now,
> A' the birds are paired and biggin';
> Saft soughin' wins dry the dubby howe,
> And the eildit puir are thiggin.

The Vale had just emerged from its severest winter buffeting in 50 years. Three feet of ice and snow had subdued the waters of the Don, drifts and wreathes had blanketed fields and hill slopes, blocked the roads, choked and halted the economy of the countryside.

Lambs had died, crops had suffered. Now it was over and the first blink of sunshine had driven away frustration and provided the eternal inspiration for renewed effort.

Six weeks and more separated the farmers from the routine they should have been following. There was a start to ploughing instead of an end to sowing.

February crocuses were late by a whole month and the snowdrops – whose bowed heads reflected exceptional bravery – gave the touches of colour that ought to have come from the bursting green on the trees and hedgetops.

But the whir of the tractors persisted far into the night and hope was stirring.

It only needed someone to talk about it and Gordon Will was the man. Mr Will was a banker. He was also a district councillor and a philosopher. So he was qualified to see it three ways.

Now he, like the rest, was content to dwell but briefly on the recent bad times and to say instead… 'In the countryside we are full of hope… full of hope and how otherwise at this time of year in such weather?'

This was the philosophy of the countryman who had lost stock, crops and time and had been all but parted from the last reserve of patience. It was the philosophy so often misconstrued by the townsman, yet so eagerly sought by the leaders of industry, business and Government while they fished for trout and salmon by the peaceful waters of the Don. It was the most elementary of all philosophies – the eternal lesson of co-operation with nature's purposes. 99

Six years later, the Rev. Samuel Devlin, Alford's Church of Scotland minister at the time, was to write in the 1953 *Third Statistical Account of Scotland,* the following account about 'The Parish of Alford':

66 The greatest change in the parish during the past 100 years has been the growth of the village of Alford. Formerly, the centre of the community was around what used to be Alford West Church: here were the church, the shop and the smithy. In 1859, however, with the completion of the railway, linking Alford with Aberdeen, there began the gradual growth of what is now the village, lying one and a half miles to the east of the former centre. The railway was closed to passenger traffic in 1950, but there is still a fairly heavy goods traffic. Today there are more shopping facilities in Alford than is normal in a village of its size. There are two bakers' shops, three garages, two chemists, two newsagents, one tailor, one shoemaker, one saddler, one jeweller, one ironmonger, one hairdresser, one furniture store and five general merchants' businesses, one of which is a Co-operative store while two are licensed.

One business, controlled by one family, includes house furnishing and removals, groceries, ironmongery, jewellery, drapery and dressmaking. Vans belonging to grocers and bakers in the village serve the parish; others come from Kemnay and some, from as far away as Aberdeen, bring fish. There are branches of the Commercial Bank, the

Clydesdale and North of Scotland Bank, and the Aberdeen Savings Bank. On Tuesday, which is market day, the village presents a lively scene with the farmer in to buy or sell, or just meet his friends, while his wife uses the occasion for shopping.

Two hotels, one of which is licensed, and two guest houses, cater for summer visitors who are numerous in the season. One must admire the skill and energy with which the people of the village cultivate their gardens in an area where late frosts are more the rule than the exception. A healthy rivalry exists between neighbours and the result is a pleasing picture of order and a creditable display of flowers and vegetables.

In 1951 the local population numbered 1,248 and a number of houses in the village still depended on an outside tap. The Farquharsons who at one time owned almost two thirds of the parish, had gone and Haughton House, their former mansion had now become a summer boarding hotel. Eggs were sent to the Donside Egg Grading Station in the village and the records show that in one week some 1,900 cases of eggs, valued at £12,000 passed through the station. The Vale of Alford Agricultural Association held an annual agricultural show which was one of the outstanding events in the parish. The tradesmen serving the parish included 2 joiners, 1 plumber and 1 painter, each of whom employed several men.

A pack of wolf cubs, with a membership of 30, meets in Alford School and there was a troop of boy scouts until recently, when unfortunately the introduction of the army cadet force depleted its membership. The various productions of the junior dramatic club have shown the value of training youth in the sphere of acting. The young people also have a tennis club, which was recently revived. Throughout the winter months the Alford Public Hall is fully used by various clubs and organisations; a badminton club meets there twice a week, various dances are held during the season and a travelling cinema visits the village once a week. An arts club, in association with the Arts Council of Great Britain, affords the people an opportunity of seeing

Alford Wolf Cubs in 1950.

and hearing first class singers, actors and instrumentalists. There are two dramatic clubs, both of which try to present one play during the winter. Alford is fortunate in having two fine parks. The Pleasure Park, opened in 1921 and paid for by funds raised by public conscription, has tennis courts, football grounds and a bowling green. Along the Montgarrie Road, near the river, is the Murray Park, given to the community by Charles Murray, along with a trust fund for its upkeep. The Vale of Alford Curling Club owns a pond in this park.

They are an industrious people, careful in the management of their affairs, with a pawky sense of humour which does much to lighten their labours. Parents are alive to their responsibility, and the standards of family life are sound, while the children are encouraged to take full advantage of the education provided. In a farming community the amount of leisure is limited, but the people take advantage of the many social events and keep in touch with the wider world through newspapers and wireless. The one policeman in the parish has little crime to deal with, most of it being of a petty nature. 99

Thus reads the relatively objective statistical report of the time, though punctuated by some revealing personal observations and references to events, persons and places with whom and with which I, my family and boyhood friends were to become directly involved.

Induction

At some point I recognised Willie Grassick as the catalyst necessary for my Donside induction – a gradual process over weekends and holidays as the seasons dictated the village loons' activities. Thus in spring I learned to guddle for trout underneath the overhanging banks and beneath the boulders of the burns; discover the nests of chaffinches, greenfinches, goldfinches and yellowhammers and watch the screeching seagulls as they trailed and plunged behind the Fergies, Massey Harris's or Fordson Majors ploughing the rich black loam of the farmlands.

All too short summer holidays found us diving into the Don, swinging from the branches of the massive 'Tarzan' tree or re-enacting Civil War, '45 Rebellion or Wild West conflicts in Haughton Woods. Shorter autumn days brought darker nights and a return to the village where the unwary pedestrian was peppered by hidden snipers pluffing streams of roddens out of sawn-off bicycle pumps from the shadows of a dimly lit Main Street. Winter snows and ice took the loons out to the delights of the 'skater' and sledging 'doon the beltie' late into the freezing evenings. Going from a 20-minute cycle ride between Mannofield and the Grammar to a one-and-a-quarter-hour daily bus commute from Alford to school in Aberdeen was a shock to the system, but initially I regarded it as a new adventure. Apart from one sharp bout of travel sickness, brought on by the all pervading smell of diesel and lurching rumble of the old Leylands, I adjusted quickly to my new mode of travel. Too embarrassed to ask the conductress to stop the bus, I threw up into my school cap, holding it tightly until I was able to heave cap and contents out of the door after the next passenger had boarded.

The route via Dunecht detoured through Cluny and dropped me outside the school gates in Albyn Place. I don't remember the bus ever being full, which, considering this was the only direct mode of transport between village and city, the train being on its last legs, indicated that the country population was still firmly rooted in local employment; though bonny Betty McCombie, daughter of butcher John McCombie, journeyed daily by train to Aberdeen High School for Girls.

While I was to continue commuting to Aberdeen over the next two years, Rory enrolled at Alford School which eased his introduction to village life. Conversely, in my Grammar School uniform, it was just a matter of time before I would be targeted as an undesirable public school alien. In the meantime I felt more secure with my Grammar School friends and I alternated stays at their homes in Aberdeen with reciprocal visits to Mayview.

After two years it was decided that I should transfer from the

Grammar School to Inverurie Academy, a mere 18 miles away. I don't remember any discussion on the subject and can only surmise that Norrie and Alice felt that the shorter bus journey would be less arduous or, more likely, less expensive. Certainly it was a considerable wrench from friends I'd known since primary school days and I would have to wait 40 years before meeting up with them again at an FP reunion in the 90s. In the meantime I had to adjust from a city grammar school to a country town co-ed secondary. It was a baptism of fire, not made any easier by 'Bessie', my new French teacher who singled me out by declaring that having come from a boys' school I was obviously not accustomed to having girls in the class. My time during that first year at Inverurie was summed up by Norrie more accurately than he knew when he wrote in one of his later poems:

'An' the loons an' the quines kept makin' coorse rhymes
Losh but ma hert wis richt sair'

By the end of the year, however, daily exposure to the unforgiving taunts of the Garioch loons and quines, no nonsense school dinners of stovies, beetroot and oatcakes, survival skills in arctic conditions on the playing fields and bus journeys where new friendships were forged amongst the Alford contingent, completed the induction which led to the happiest and most privileged formative years of a lifetime.

Yokin'

aving settled in, Norrie and Alice took stock of the upset in the hitherto regulated pattern of their city lives. Initially they still depended on their Aberdeen friends for any sort of social outlet, largely denied to them in a North-East village which viewed incomers with wariness, laced with anticipation at the stimulating brew of gossip which they might provide. And in this they were not to be disappointed.

Norrie's commuting hardships, not to mention white collar status, became a thing of the past as, clutching the remnants of his toast and Keillers thick cut marmalade, a cup of tea and the P&J, he would shuffle purposefully in his carpet slippers from the kitchen to the bank in time to admit Nancy Grassick, his single clerical assistant, for a relaxed start at 10 a.m. Apart from Tuesdays when, amidst a cacophony of drovers' shouts, despairing bellows and plaintive bleats, the livestock sales took place at the end of the garden, Norrie had little to keep himself occupied beyond recording in careful copperplate hand, within their green ASB-embossed bankbooks, the modest deposits of his daily handful of canny clientele. If Tuesday's regular upsurge in business might, in his waking dreams, herald a run on the bank and a stampede of bankbook-waving depositors from beyond the Howe, Norrie did not let the pressure get to him. The P&J, with its world and national news, pawky local comment and daily crossword, must have helped him retain his sanity as he went about his business, preserving the financial confidentialities of his fellow citizens.

Dependence on occasional visits from their social circle in Aberdeen only put off the need to integrate with their new village neighbours. Clearly they had to listen, learn and perhaps drop the odd hint on how they might contribute to the community of which they had become an unwitting part.

The 'Digging for Victory' wartime philosophy, coupled with having lived next to allotments in Mannofield and now finding himself in the heart of an agricultural community, prompted Norrie to demonstrate that white collar workers could adapt to the world of the dungaree. Accordingly trenches dug in the rich loam were soon producing huge crops of celery which, despite appearing at every meal, failed to convert his offspring to a healthy diet of fresh home grown produce. In addition his yoghurt bacteriology project involved jars of Quatermass-like lumps of culture bubbling away to produce a revolting cloudy liquid which Norrie religiously drank each morning. This indulgence in products alien to his family, far from helping their integration into the village, sowed the seeds of suspicion amongst the populace that their new Savings Bank manager 'wis jist nae wise'.

The Stalag Luft free-range chicken scheme, however,

Fa said the McCombies wis feel?

Ma dad bocht a car frae a fairmer,
Fa lived at the back o' the howe.
He paid thirty pounds for the carcass
An' a spare tied on wi' some tow.

'Twis a gey muckle car, nae a mini,
A dizen horses were yokit inside.
It wis a' pentit green, far the rust
   didnae show;
We wis fair dementit wi' pride.

We kent fine fit fouk wid be sayin',
The McCombies wis gypit an' feel,
But us wi' a car, losh we'd
   show them;
The McCombies wis deein'
   gey weel.

It stairtit a' richt wi' the button,
The brakes were haudin' as weel.
Coorse wi' the petrol?
   Fit d'ye expect?
Fa said the McCombies wis feel?

An' fan we fun oot fit the catch v
It's a mercy', said dad, 'we're
   nae deid'.
It grew unco thrang an' the
   steerin' gaed wrang
Fanever he wrocht tae get speed.

It sure wis the speak o' the villag
The McCombies wis caught
   oot aince mair,
An' the loons an' the quines
   kept makin' coorse rhymes;
Losh, but ma hert wis richt sair.

But Dad hid some tools in
   the sheddie,
An' I kent for some wark he wis
For I saw by the gey thrawn look
   in his een
The McCombies wisnae licket
   as yet.

ultimately convinced the village wiseacres that 'nae wise' should be downgraded to 'feel'. Ironically, here was an idea which the whole family embraced with enthusiasm. It involved the building of a chicken run down one side of the garden and the conversion of one of the outhouses to a shed in which the chickens could lay their eggs contentedly. Deep holes were dug at intervals and poles, steadied by close-packed stones, inserted into the ground. Chicken wire up to a height of six feet was attached to the poles and 'losh be here' the chicken run was

He work't an' I wis soon helpin'
A' through the long afternoon,
An' fan it grew dark, we went
   on wi' the wark,
An' loused by the licht o'
   the moon.

But we loused wi' herts that
   were lichtsome,
For the faut we'd found an' l
   aid bare:
The drivin' shaft wis richt
   oot o' line,
An' dirled at speed gey sair.

Weel we sorted that oot but
   still didnae stop
For the hale o' the week an
   some mair.
We strippit' an' cleaned an' iled
   an' greased
An' pit a'thing back wi' great care.

An' fan wi' fun oot, aye in secret,
That a'thing wis workin' gae weel,
Wi' scrapit an' pentit the hale
   car ower;
Fa' said the McCombies wis feel?

Fa said the McCombies wis feel?
Fa said the McCombies wis gypit?
Oor car wis the best in the
   parish syne,
An' hid a' the new anes lickit.

But noo wi' the price o' petrol,
Ye ken fu' weel fit it's like,
The car's been laid up in
   the sheddie,
An' Dad's gone back tae the bike.

An' naebody wints tae buy a car
As aul' as forty nine;
The McCombies wis feel in
   the first place,
An' the McCombies are still
   oot o' line.

complete. Half a dozen chickens were purchased and the family settled down to daily fresh eggs and perhaps foreby a fattened fowl for Christmas. Pregnant inhabitants of the chicken shed were provided with cosy straw lined semi-detached nesting boxes and roosts from which they could compare maternity notes.

It was at this point that things went horribly wrong. For some reason the expectant mothers elected to ignore their maternity suites and lay their eggs from the roosts. Had the family been warned we could have held a frying pan under an imminent layer. Denied their daily egg ration, the family demanded revenge in the shape of a freshly dispatched plump chicken for the table. Under the critical eyes of his three sons, Norrie finally cornered the victim and prepared to administer the *coup de grace* by standing on the ends of a poker laid across the poor creature's neck, grabbing its body and pulling upwards. Far from being put out of its suffering, the demented bird broke free and ran with lolling neck hither and thither until it finally succumbed to the blow of an axe.

Norrie's decision to acquire a car had absolutely nothing to do with status; more a practical need to maintain contact with the outside world. The limited means at his disposal – he was initially being paid more than it was worth to manage the branch – dictated that it was always going to be a vintage job, though no collector's item. An old Austin was duly purchased for £40 from a farmer – who probably couldn't believe his luck – and so Norrie redeemed himself in the eyes of Alice and the boys by finally acquiring the sort of social trapping associated with someone of professional standing. In later years, having finally converted from urban to rural mode, he was to mark this conversion through poetry and prose, often in the Doric.

Alford

Opposite Mayview and sufficiently set back from the road to avoid dwarfing the family's new home, stood the sombre granite pile of James Coutts & Sons' emporium, hub of the Gordon family grocery, clothing, jewellery, hardware, painting, decorating and furnishing empire. From here radiated the variegated fleet o weel kent maroon vans across the Howe and beyond, bumping up farm tracks to remote dwellings at the end of lonely Highland glens, from Dornoch in the east to Ullapool in the west. Whether beds for your nuptial encounters or 'safety preens' for the nappies, consequent on your success therein, the Gordons catered for every conceivable need. Even their clocks and calendars, marking the passage of time in parlours and kitchens throughout the vale, indicated when it 'micht be aboot time tae gie the best room a licky o' pent an' foreby maybe some floory like wallpaper fan Beldie gets mairrit next spring'.

In his poem *Monopoly*, Norrie celebrates an early concept of the present hypermarket culture in which it is not too difficult

Tae mak' ye skirl an' use yer lungs,
The midwife gies yer dowp a skelp;
Ye're newly born but sune ye'll find,
'Twas only wi' McKerrow's help.

Pram an' bath, twa kinds o' nappy,
Talcum poother an' preens galore;
The whisky tae keep yer faither happy,
Wis a' got frae McKerrow's store.

The grocer's, the dairy, the butcher's,
    the mill,
The painter's, the jiner's, the chemist's
    shop;
Ye wint tae buy or wint a job?
McKerrow's yer man, he owns the lot.

An' efter 'oors it's juist the same,
McKerrow's still the boss, ye'll find;

Chairman here or chairman ther
O' sports and clubs o' every kind

Aye, wark for him an' tak' yer pay
Yer leisure 'oors (unpaid) are still
The same as through yer workin'
Subject tae McKerrow's will.

An' even fan he disnae choose,
Tae chair a club for ony reason;
The chairman there just need na
McKerrow draps a word in seaso

An' fan ye tire o' this an' dee,
An' gang at last afore yer maker;
McKerrow still has wark tae dae,
Remember he's the undertaker.

Alford Stores

A Hairst Tae Min' On

to discern his model.

Next door to Mayview the kind and gentle Donald Gillies ran the best sweet shop in town. Shelves buckled under the weight of jars stuffed to the neck with a mouth-watering selection of liquorice allsorts, toffees and multi-coloured boiled sweets. Threepenny bars of McCowan's 'coo candy' were not only guaranteed to last throughout the day, but painlessly remove lingering first teeth at a single chew, while the ubiquitous pandrop or 'kirk sooker' helped soothe the stresses induced by ranting Sunday morning sermons.

Only problem was for a youngster to attract Donald's attention from the latest gossip with his adult clientele. These conversations often lasted so long that customers frequently left the shop having forgotten what they came in for in the first place. On one occasion Rory attempted to claim refunds on

Gordon's fleet of vans

Donald Gillies today

lemonade bottles which he had retrieved from crates stored in
Donald's shed behind the shop. Sadly, this ended with a painful
confession to Donald under Norrie's direction and an early
introduction to financial management, based on a repayment
plan funded by reducing Rory's pocket money.

Along from Donald's was the small chemist's run by the
Misses Alexander, best remembered for performing for Rory in
their genteel, net-curtained drawing room, a duet with
pianoforte accompaniment, entitled *Rise up Rory darling for they're
knocking at the door...*

Opposite, stood Gordon's painting and decorating outlet,

better known as 'Peter Duncan's' after the friendly manager who ran the shop. Rumour had it that Peter once sold half a dozen tins of different coloured paints to young Royan Ellis of Crookmore who had been sent into the village by the grieve to buy some tartan paint.

Beyond the station, Gordon's furniture store and the garage run by Isle of Man local celebrities and brothers, Alan and Jock Smith, commerce petered out towards the eastern end of the long Main Street which ran from the East Kirk on the other side, past a row of detached villas and the Station Garage, to finish at the Fountain in front of easily the village's most imposing building, the Haughton Arms Hotel, jewel of the Spence dynasty. To the right of the Fountain, Bridge Road carried on to Brig of Alford and Montgarrie, while to the left, Kingsford and Greystone Roads branched off to the village hall and school respectively.

The real centre of village activity, however, lay along Main Street between Mayview and the Fountain, reflecting even then its relative prosperity, based on the railway and the rich, surrounding farmlands. While the Clydesdale and Commercial Banks provided business backing for their farming customers, the ubiquitous Aberdeen Savings Bank managed the saving aspirations of the less financially well endowed.

William Valentine butcher in the deep freeze

Also within the village hub, Alford boasted two butchers — one, the local McCombie's, the other a branch of the Valentine chain. Between them was Stewart's the baker, run by the rangy and somewhat abrupt Simpson Stewart, from whose premises alluring aromas of fresh bread drifted out into the chill, early morning air.

On the corner, opposite the Fountain, stood the Co-op for all household goods and general provisions. The Co-op it was that pioneered television sales in the village, and Norrie, who must have had a rush of blood to the head, was one of their early customers. Nerve jangling excitement and anticipation greeted the installation of the neat, veneered box with its goldfish bowl screen ready to bring Britain, its people and their doings into our very own front room. Despite frantic efforts with the horizontal and vertical controls, however, all we got on the screen was a blizzard, epic even by North-East standards. Back to the Co-op and within a week came the promised new set, fresh from its Dundee warehouse – or so we were reliably informed by local manager John Yeats. Sadly, and unbeknown to John, Norrie had slyly marked the original model and swiftly discovered that the replacement was in fact the original. Reverse rush of blood to the head and back to radio's *The Goons, Journey into Space, Dick Barton* and *The McFlannels*.

Next to the Co-op the hyperactive Jock Milne ran the newsagents and, as an afterthought, cropped hair for those with a predilection for tonsures. These were mainly children who had no choice in the matter. Jock's shop was a delight for kids who suffered from incessant parental nagging to tidy their rooms. It was a cheerful shambles within which Jock pirouetted like a Dervish as he frantically dispensed everything from 'frenchies' and fags, to the latest editions of the P&J and, on Saturday nights, the eagerly awaited *Green Final* with its football reports. Like Donald Gillies, though from an entirely different school, Jock was one of Alford's memorable characters. Married to the imposing Bet, squeezed behind the shop counter with a fag suspended from her lips and a faintly contemptuous expression, Jock was up at crack of dawn to collect the papers from the first bus out of Aberdeen and was last in the village to close up shop.

A little further down on the other side, licensed grocer Royan's catered for more epicurean tastes. Next to Royan's, Nicholas Simpson, the diminutive chemist, peered over his spectacles and kept his confidentialities to himself. His premises occupied as they still do, the original site of William Hay & Sons Ltd, once the North-East's own soft drinks company. Across from Simpson's and next to Valentines was the modest shop of Adam Reid, the Glasgow-trained bespoke tailor who crafted two striking tweed suits for Norrie, one of which, a Norfolk jacket with matching breeches, was later consigned to the wardrobe of my local amateur dramatic society in Kent from whence it emerged for 19th century period plays.

More or less in the centre of the village stood the post office run by husband and wife team, Mr and Mrs Robbie. A modest establishment barely distinguishable from the row of cottages of which it formed a part, the post office was, nevertheless, the nerve centre for the village and wider community. While the dapper Mr Robbie rejoiced in his official title of postmaster, everyone knew that plump, kindly and quietly efficient Mrs Robbie was the brains behind a smooth running and contented workforce of posties and counter staff. I never quite understood where Mr Robbie fitted into the postal equation, though he was frequently to be seen greeting the local folk while he exercised his Scottie along Main Street, until one winter when it suddenly disappeared. Weeks later as the thick, drifting blankets of snow receded from the surrounding fields, some of us loons came across the frozen body of the wee craitur in an icy burn under a ledge of overhanging snow and brought the sad news back to the Robbies.

Later, as an impecunious student, I was befriended by Mrs Robbie to deliver telegrams on Sundays and after business hours to anywhere within a five-mile radius of the village. A memorable assignment took place one Sunday, again in the grip of winter, when I cycled, with Post Office armband and telegram, way beyond the 'Brig' and up a long, winding and precipitous track to a farm which might as well have been inhabited by Sherpas. In the teeth of freezing snow flurries and icy underfoot conditions, I finally arrived at the front door hoping for the offer of something warming, only to have the telegram swiftly acknowledged and the door unceremoniously slammed in my face. At Christmas I was drafted in to help with parcel deliveries. Legs dangling from the tailgate of the little Royal Mail van, I leapt off and on as we hurtled round the village, dropping off our Christmas goodies.

Two other establishments on the fringe of the village need mention. The first on the Montgarrie road just beyond the 'English' church was a wooden structure in which Jimmy Ingles

Alford Secondary 3 in 1956

school, it is felt that the school at Alford could well be elevated to the status of a senior secondary school, thus reducing the amount of travelling by the scholars. The school has an excellent canteen, built in 1947, which provides a two course meal for 6d; it also provides meals for the neighbouring schools at Craigievar, O'Neil Corse, Keig and Tullynessle, and in all, an average of 400 meals a day is prepared. The introduction of school meals has been of great benefit to the children, the improvement in their physical appearance being quite noticeable. 🙶

Alford Secondary 3 in 1957.

Robin Adair's earlier *Weekly Journal* feature also contains nostalgic pictures of Alford School primary and secondary pupils shown in science, woodwork and needlework classes.

The same feature gives a fascinating insight into contemporary views expressed by pupils and their dominie, Mr Ritchie, on the raising of the school leaving age from 14 to 15. Adair writes...

❝Up the hill to Alford School I walked with several of the new school population... each one studiously non-committal and slightly suspicious about the raising of the school leaving age that has now become a fact.

One said something about a job he'd missed; another about an opening at a commercial college in Aberdeen.

Most of the parents had accepted the additional year as a sound investment; some had felt the blow to the domestic economy.

Mr Ritchie, the headmaster, knew that his teachers worked for the

Alford School football team

Presentation to Mr Ritchie at the prizegiving in 1954

benefit of the pupils, not so that they may have a better job at fifteen – for the jobs a-going would be just the same – but because additional knowledge makes for fuller living.

I shall be happy if we can help the children to become more self-reliant, more expressive, more appreciative – not only of art, music and literature but of the ordinary things in life, the true values and the fundamental issues.

Mr Ritchie did not hesitate to say that many of the pupils who hurried from school at 14 were only partially educated. Another year at school would not make for a new Jerusalem, but for less wastage and greater opportunity. 99

Dominie Ritchie was succeeded by dominie Baxter who was to bring an even more rigorous approach to discipline within Alford School, and segregation of the sexes. Separating the boys' and girls' playgrounds was an iron railing over which pubescent youth dared to associate with the opposite sex. At an assembly designed to erase any verbal communication, erotic or otherwise, between loons and quines, the dominie concluded his ranting

Mr Ritchie's retirement

diatribe against his sinful charges with the anti-climatic words 'and now we'll have a prayer'.

Within this regime, the ethics of sportsmanship were robustly upheld by PE teacher Cyril Mutch, who belted minister's son John Begg, the school goalie, for graciously stepping aside to let the opposition score a consolation goal, after the Alford team had trounced them.

Twenty-odd years later Alford School, under new rector Robert Graham, entered the brave new world of comprehensive education; it became an Academy and admitted its first fifth year class of some twenty boys and girls. In September 1972, under the heading of *A New Start at Alford*, well known columnist Cuthbert Graham wrote thoughtfully in the P&J's WEEKEND REVIEW...

❝ With a present role of 261, the secondary school at Alford must

Alford School football team – winners of Aberdeen Schools
Under-15s five-a-side competition 1955. They are Ernest Murray,
Mike Barron, George Esson, John McCombie and Bill Christie.

School   51 surely be the smallest in Scotland. Yet it fulfils all the criteria laid down by the educational theorists. Around 70 pupils are starting their secondary schooling in a fully comprehensive common course. This means that all of them will have exactly the same chance without streaming and the segregation of academic and non academic...

The comprehensive academy at Alford serves the whole of upper Donside from Monymusk to Corgarff, and a lateral area that reaches north to Keig and Lumsden and south to O'Neil Corse. The good folk of Monymusk felt that Alford was less their natural service centre than Inverurie – but they were happy for their children to go to Alford with its superb new school buildings and smaller numbers.

There is just one snag about Alford as compared with, say, Peterhead or Fraserburgh. As it is the centre of a completely rural area, job opportunities close to their homes are more limited for the school leavers, and contact with the realities of an industrialised civilisation is more remote.

Strenuous efforts to overcome these handicaps will be made. One idea is that there should be more regular – perhaps even weekly – contact days when pupils from Alford meet the pupils of other Aberdeenshire academies, not merely for sporting encounters on the football field or badminton court, but also in discussion groups for the exchange of ideas, attitudes and experiences.

But there is another side to the medal. Who can measure the value, in a spiritual sense, or even in practical sense of growing up in a country environment?

I like the story of the countrywoman who, although she had thrown away her schoolbag 70 years ago, was shocked by the idea that modern boys and girls went to distant schools by bus.

'Just think what they miss!' she exclaimed. 'No real contact with nature! No sappy sookers for them to cut! No birds, no bees, no flowers! No adventures by stile and hedgerow. No paddling in the burn and pu'ing the gowans fine'. She was appalled.

There is still a reminder of that other life in the vestibule of the

Weekend Review

THIS IS MY COUNTRY

A New Start at Alford

By CUTHBERT GRAHAM
With pictures by IAN HARDIE

Weel-bunkered links, a pirtney loan,
A puff isn't aa the hin'most greens—
Ay, but it's fine hoo dreams conteive
To gie guid golfers back their drive . . .
—CHARLES MURRAY

IT'S A TIME of new beginnings in the Vale of Alford. This month some twenty boys and girls formed the first fifth year class in Alford School — now without a qualification Alford Academy.

At the same time Haughton House picnic area and caravan site came into being, and 100 cars from Aberdeen and elsewhere came to funnel the new amenity and savour the beauties of a splendid rendezvous in a country house setting.

What would Charles Murray think of this? I am pretty sure it would rejoice his heart.

That Alford should have its own fully comprehensive secondary school is something that gives me particular pleasure. For once the idea of size and centralisation has a few challenge. And this is a significant portent for the future.

With a present roll of 261, the secondary school at Alford must surely be the smallest in Scotland. Yet it fulfils all the criteria laid down by the educational theorists. Around 70 pupils are starting their secondary schooling in a fully comprehensive common course. This means that all of them will have exactly the same chance without streaming and the appreciation of academic and non-academic.

The educational advantages of small classes will be their and no one realises this more keenly that the new Rector of the Academy, Mr Robert Graham, who tells me that he has proved this in a personal way, through the experience of his own children who came from Hamilton (with classes of 50) to Alford (with classes of 25).

Serving all the Upper Don

The comprehensive academy at Alford serves the whole of upper Donside from Monymusk to Corgarff, and a catchment area that reaches north to Keig and Lumsden and south to O'Neil-Corse. The good folk of Monymusk felt that Alford was less their natural service centre than Inverurie—but they were happy for their children to go to Alford with its superior new school buildings and smaller numbers.

There is just one snag about Alford as compared with say Peterhead or Fraserburgh. As it is the centre of a completely rural area, job opportunities close to their homes are more limited for the school leavers, and contact with the realities of an industrialised civilisation is more remote of course, but also in discussion groups for the exchange of ideas, attitudes and experiences.

But there is another side to the medal. Who can measure the value, in a spiritual sense, or even in practical sense of growing up in a country environment?

I like the story of the countrywoman who left school about 70 years ago. Though she had thrown her schoolbags away for the last time all these years ago she was shocked by the idea that modern boys and girls went to distant schools by bus.

"Just think what they miss!" she exclaimed. "No real contact with nature! No canny neukers for them to curl! No birds, no bees, no flowers! No adventures by stile and bridge and burn. No puddling in the burn and prying the gowans fine" she was appalled.

There is still a reminder of that older life in the vestibule of the school at Alford, where R. O. Robertson's wood carving of "the Whistler," Hamewith's wee herd lad, stands blowing "rants sae lively" on an admittedly rather abstract whistle. The urban boy may be a step ahead in the materialistic rat race, but like the wee herd he may also miss "the craggit heron nabbin' puddocks in the seggs".

NOW TURN TO PAGE SEVEN.

Mr Robert Graham, Rector of Alford Academy, on the roof of the four-storey secondary teaching block, which gives a magnificent view of the village and the Vale of Alford, with the outline of Bennachie in the background. On his right, below, can be seen the games hall, the administrative block and the primary school, with the community centre and Alford Branch Library behind. The lower picture shows a view of the busy Main Street of Alford. This month Alford Academy was launched on its career as a fully comprehensive senior secondary school, with a fifth year class of around 20 and a common course for the 71 entrants in the first year of the secondary school. It taps pupils from Monymusk in the east to Corgarff in the west, O'Neil Corse on the south and Keig and Lumsden on the north.

ILLUSTRATION COURTESY OF ABERDEEN JOURNALS

school at Alford, where R. O. Robertson's wood carving of *The Whistler*, Hamewith's wee herd lad, stands blowing 'rants sae lively'. The urban boy may be a step ahead in the materialistic rat race, but like the wee herd he may also miss 'the craggit heron nabbin' puddocks in the seggs'. 🙶

School

53

Until then, Inverurie Academy was a daily 36-mile round bus trip for Alford scholars who aspired to post-15 education. Twelve miles further up the Don, Strathdon scholars were billeted in Inverurie, returning home only at weekends. Alford and Strathdon apart, the Academy recruited from a wide range of Garioch farms and communities.

The bus crews were all Alford based, in particular May McCombie, the conductress; the Harper twins, Sandy Turriff and Dod Watt, the drivers. May was a no nonsense lady who ruled her bus with a force of personality which made you feel privileged to be given a ticket. Stood on the middle step by the concertina doors when she wasn't backed up against the one fan heater in the bus, she surveyed the road ahead much as a captain surveys the ocean from his bridge. Her tailored black Alexander's tunic, skirt (breeks in winter) and cap, together with overlapping bandolier supporting her silver ticket machine served to emphasise the unchallenged authority which nobody would have had the nerve to challenge in the first place. Sandy was to be remembered for entirely filling a cab designed for a man half his size, only emerging when the bus buried itself in a snow drift and then urging his passengers to grab a shovel from the boot and start digging themselves out. Although Sandy's exhortations worked well on the homeward run of the scholars' bus from Inverurie, they failed miserably on the morning run to the Academy. That having been said, we made it through most of the time, the only major exception being the great gale of 1953 when in a single night whole forests were reduced to matchwood, roads became inaccessible and the landscape

Lily Simpson with Dod Watt

changed beyond recognition

The scholars' bus to Inverurie started at Keig, continued through Montgarrie and arrived in Alford at the ungodly hour of 7.50am. This might just have been acceptable during the summer months, but in winter made unacceptable demands on the half asleep, frozen scholars huddled together for warmth in the rear of the vehicle.

Mind you, if I had problems with the bus stop just across the road, spare a thought for the Law loons from East Cevidley in the backwoods of Keig, and others like them, who had to struggle down snowy farm tracks in sub-zero temperatures to reach the bus. Opaque windows and steaming breath added to the igloo interior in which thawing out was a joke, while the conductress, jamming her tightly-breeked bum firmly against the heater, prevented any chance of diesel driven warm air permeating the vehicle. Still, you had the option of warming up by digging the bus out of snow drifts or simply freezing to death.

Despite all their privations, however, the camaderie between the Alford, Montgarrie and Keig scholars as they joked, gossiped, scribbled and copied last minute homework made the daily commute more than bearable in their final years of schooling. It was at this time that I decided my future career was in journalism and, using Norrie's office as a publishing base, typed out three carbon copies of a weekly newsletter which I distributed amongst my fellow students on the morning run. How long the fledgling publication lasted, what I wrote about or whether my readers cared have all been lost in time.

Local character Wullie 'Speedy' Mitchell was the one passenger who used the scholars' bus from Alford to Kintore where he worked in a watchmaker's shop. Speedy suffered from indigestion for which he was prescribed charcoal biscuits, barely distinguishable from lumps of compressed coal dust. These he generously offered around, demonstrating their efficacy as he noisily munched his way through the contents of a brown paper bag. His offer was never taken up.

About six miles short of Inverurie the bus picked up the Kemnay contingent of scholars. Regarded by their up-country contemporaries as the 'rougher' element, the Kemnay crowd thought much the same about the hill billies from the Howe. They tended to sit apart, the Kemnay lot occupying the front and the Alford group the rear of the bus until, that is, shy adolescent glances began to give way to the first flickerings of innocent romance between the odd loon and quine of both communities.

The Alford bus finally rolled into the square in front of Inverurie's Town Hall about 8.40am. There its occupants joined the throng of scholars as they poured off buses from the other outlying villages and farmlands of the Garioch, mingling in turn with their fellows from the town, and suddenly the lane leading from the square to the school swelled with raw-faced, blazered North-East youth sometimes edging uncertainly, or striding out confidently towards the last years of compulsory education and the unknown beyond.

In 1959, eleven years after their arrival in Alford, Norrie and Alice moved to Inverurie following Norrie's promotion to the

Inverurie branch of Aberdeen Savings Bank; ten years later, in 1969, Norrie wrote an article on Inverurie for the *Scots Magazine*'s September edition. Forty years on, some interesting comparisons can be made with his observations on the town.

66 Without the locos, Inverurie would be just another sleepy market town. The Great North of Scotland Railway Company… built houses to accommodate all the workers. The works manager was given a large, handsome house in spacious grounds, his departmental heads were settled in semi-detached villas with ample gardens, and foremen, tradesmen and unskilled were all housed in such a way as to show the status of each group.

This influx became known as 'The Colony' and although these newcomers soon ceased to be strangers, the colony remains.

Just over ten years ago, the first threat of closure affected these workshops. As a result, many young men left the town for places such as Corby and Swindon or emigrated overseas.

Throughout the town, traffic has been tidied up and adequate parking space provided. So much so that, every weekend, shoppers come from Aberdeen to park with ease, shop in comfort and then enjoy a meal in hotels where the customer is still made very welcome.

With the greatly enlarged Academy in its midst, the burgh is now the educational centre for a very wide area. Retired people are happy to live within this town of ideal size… Within two years Inverurie expects its housing needs to be fully satisfied.

The new houses are not glorified boxes, but well-built houses in a variety of design, set in landscaped schemes and including ambitious provision for the aged. Inverurie people have raised much money by voluntary effort and are looking forward to starting to build a swimming pool this summer.

Norrie concluded:

A satellite town may be the right size and shape but, until the people make it theirs and take it over, it will be but another sadness where the night wind blows the paper litter around the shopping centre. Where the starveling trees die in their concrete pots and a fountain fails to run. And 'they' will be too distant and too nebulous to blame. 99

Whatever else may have been transpiring in this bustling agricultural and industrial centre, to the Garioch scholars of the time, Inverurie meant the Academy and its renowned rector, Dr Norman Dixon. Personally I have yet to meet any more inspired and respected school head than Dr Dixon, remembered with deep affection by all those generations of scholars privileged to have passed through his hands. An imposing personality who strode through the corridors, his academic gown billowing behind him, Dr Dixon had an intimate knowledge of all his charges.

In my final year, and somewhat full of myself as a sixth form prefect, I was approached at speed by the revered Doctor who exclaimed as he swept past, 'and how is my gay young Lothario today?' Readers will appreciate that in these more innocent times the rector was not referring to my sexual orientation, but rather my tendency to think of myself as a good time guy. At the time, however, I didn't know what he was talking about and lost no time in checking out Lothario in the classical reference dictionary. To this day I am still mystified as to how he could possibly have cracked my carefully disguised alter ego.

While present day educationalists might well frown at the rector's rewards and punishments policy, it certainly made an impact at the time. Following major examinations throughout the school, the marked scripts were tremulously scanned by the nervous examinees to discover whether the boldly pencilled 'See me' or 'Please see me' appeared alongside the marks at the top of their papers. In short, every paper had undergone the rector's scrutiny, the top scorers receiving the coveted 'Please see me' accolade, while those with the dreaded 'See me' were left to contemplate their inevitable fate at the end of the rector's tawse.

Over the course of the following days, two queues of scholars formed up outside the rector's office, one attempting to conceal their smugness; the other attempting to convey an impression of bravado. Whatever this may or may not have achieved in the long term, corporal punishment concentrated the mind wonderfully as part of the educational armoury.

We all retain memories of our academic mentors, and I was delighted to find that Douglas Prosser, my former English teacher at Aberdeen Grammar, had been appointed as Head of English at my new school. It was to Mr Prosser in no small measure that I owed my decision to become an English teacher. Other teachers at the Academy still spring to mind, their nicknames recalled more readily than their own names – Farney Dick, Hughie, Tommy, Algy, the Mekon, Gauldie, Bessie, Ma Bain, Bunny…

Each day started with assembly led by the rector and lusty renditions of hymns we'd all learned by heart through the years, crashed out on the piano by lanky music teacher Roland (Suicide) Smith of the flowing blond locks and bi-focal glasses. You didn't mess with Roland, whose trigger-happy reputation with the belt ensured that every class sang as though they were auditioning for the Glasgow Orpheus Choir. At one school concert in the Town Hall, the senior choir were to perform a medley of Scottish songs, conducted by Roland. Like many professional musicians, Roland was not averse to the occasional dram and had clearly imbibed one or three at the Butcher's Arms before taking his place on a podium at the edge of the stage. Throughout the performance we were hypnotised by our swaying conductor whom we expected at any moment to land up in the front row of the audience.

But the real talk o' the toon was the scandal when Roland ran off to Glasgow with one of his music pupils, the gorgeous 15-year-old daughter of a local café owner. The overwhelming reaction from us loons was how he'd managed to seduce her in the face of intense competition from every lust- driven youth in the school.

Highlights of the day for most scholars were all about feeding their faces, not with the junk food of today, but hot Scotch pies and luscious jam-filled doughnuts made by Grays the baker in West High Street. How pupils were not mown down as they stampeded across the busy High Street in pre-lollipop crossing days, I'll never know – not that a school crossing patrol would have made much impact in stemming the ravenous tide anyway.

School dinners were the next opportunity to stoke up before the long afternoon's lessons and the journey home. The young and lovely Miss Laeburn, fresh from Aberdeen's College of Domestic Science (better known as 'Dough School') presided over a kitchen of red-faced wifies, steaming cauldrons and glowing ovens. None of your healthy salads and five portions of fruit and veg per day stuff, but good, honest mince and tatties wi' skirlie, thick broths, stews, stovies and oatcakes wi' beetroot, jam sponges and dumpling covered in custard… and so to sleep, perchance to dream, slumped over desks as the teachers droned on and learning took a back seat for the rest of the day.

Unless, that is, you had games. Enter Gordon 'Killer' Killicoat and his ruthless Gulag PE team. Having been brought up in a rugby school with civilised sports pavilion, changing rooms and hot showers, football in Inverurie's pleasure park without even the basic amenities was never going to be a pleasure. I ran about aimlessly, fell over, got covered in mud and heartily hated the whole business.

The ultimate misery was games afternoon in winter. Driven mercilessly into the conifer groves bordering the pitches by PE staff recruited from Siberian teacher training colleges, we forcibly disrobed, clambered into inadequate sports gear, and hung our clothes on the branches. On our return to the pleasure park's sylvan changing facilities, the act of donning our frozen clothing was akin to levering yourself into a suit of medieval armour. Only on the homeward bus did we start to thaw out as the steam rose from our rigid shirts and the windows ran with the resultant condensation. I didn't fare much better at cricket, never understanding why a particularly pointless and boring English game should be on the Scottish PE curriculum.

But Christmas was something else, when the staff dolled themselves up and served dinner to the scholars in their final Highers year, at the annual dinner and dance. Leading up to this momentous occasion were the dances held by each of the four school houses – Urie, Balquhain, Kinkell and Harlaw. A couple of weeks before these events, the male and female PE departments combined to instruct their charges in the mysteries of ballroom and Scottish country dancing. Strung out down each side of the gym, loons and quines faced each other uncertainly until the Red Guard moved into action and the boys were driven forcibly across the floor to confront their equally apprehensive partners.

And one, two, three, one two, three, we were off, each pair holding themselves stiffly at arm's length and avoiding each other's eyes as they stared fixedly at the floor, nervous systems in shock, unable to co-ordinate the leaden movement of their black-plimsolled feet. But, wow, despite the uncompromising start, physical contact with the opposite sex was officially approved, and when the girls made their shy appearances, unrecognisable in their party dresses, at the house dances, adolescence suddenly looked a lot brighter.

The senior male scholars attended to their own unofficial adolescent development at Les Auld's. Les ran a confectioner and tobacconist shop at the corner of West High Street and the Square and this became our 'hangout' at lunchtimes and after school. Here, in the days before shopkeepers were held responsible for selling cigarettes to those under age, we got our daily nicotine fix through five Woodbines dispensed in economically viable paper packs. And for those unable to raise the odd bob a pack, Les was happy to sell you one fag at a time. Swigging coke and dragging deeply on our 'woodies', we discussed such intellectual topics as the Dons, the latest hits, and quines, with Les only too ready to offer his input to the mature and

Inverurie Academy school photo. The author is in the back row, third from the left.

sophisticated discussion initiated by his youn clientele.

So, down through the generations, Les played his part in that strange and exciting transition between adolescence and adulthood.

Kirk

C entral to village communities in the Fifties, certainly in the North-East, was the kirk, and Alford was no exception. The village boasted three churches – the East and West Presbyterian Kirks and the Scottish Episcopalian 'English' St Andrews Church. While the East Kirk and St Andrews were within the village proper, the West Kirk was a couple of miles out along the Muir of Fowlis road. The East Kirk and its manse presented their bleak and architecturally unimaginative granite frontages to the Main Street above which they stood, while the softer, less imposing St Andrews and its manse, surrounded by trees, offered a more welcoming aspect.

But the considerably smaller Auld or West Kirk was my favourite, its church yard 'where the rude forefathers of the hamlet' slept, enclosing amongst others, the graves of William Hay of lemonade fame, Stewarts the bakers, the Spence hotelier family and iconic local poet, Charles Murray. Although its exterior was simple, the atmospheric interior with its traditional balcony rising above the ground floor and the pulpit suspended somewhere between the two, allowed the Rev. Robert Begg to dominate his congregation in fiery Presbyterian style. His piercing eyes were on the same level as our little gang of four seated in the front pew of the balcony, reducing us to dumb and trembling compliance. I have a lasting image of Rev. Begg, seen through Mayview's front room bay window one evening, striding over hard-packed snow into the teeth of a vicious north-easterly blizzard, silhouetted for a moment under the street lamp opposite, his black cape streaming out behind him as he fought his way home after a visit to one of his parishioners.

Norrie's cheerful atheism excluded him from the weekly soul cleansing process, but that did not put Rev. Begg off one bit and he was a regular and welcome caller at Mayview during his village rounds. Norrie loved a good argument, theological or otherwise, and the two men were happy to respect each other's stance. Alice, on the other hand, remained steadfast in her belief although she went along with Norrie's premise that infant baptism was a pointless exercise if the squalling bairns didn't have a clue as to what was going on.

We boys dutifully attended Sunday school and church into our teens. At one point I even defected to the 'English church' where I sang in the choir with my pals, all of us enjoying the attention of the small congregation. They were not fooled by our solemn entry wearing surplices and contrite expressions, as we destroyed the illusion by fidgeting and giggling in our pews throughout the vicar's sermon. Later, at the age of 17, I decided to be baptised by Rev. Begg's predecessor, the Rev. Samuel Devlin, who took me through the required programme in the week leading up to the ceremony at the East Kirk. Alone with the minister, before the barely lit altar in an empty, darkened church with a gale blowing outside, I still retain a strong image of the experience, so I guess Norrie did have a point.

Doctor

The kirk had no monopoly on the intimacies and frailties of its faithful. Together with the village doctors, it protected the confidentialities of those whose circumstances, unfortunate or otherwise, were nobody else's business. Together, too, they participated in the ultimate mysteries of life and death as they eased new lives into the world and old ones out of it.

Dr Raymond Hilton, formerly of Bradford, arrived in Alford via Aberdeen where he had recently studied for his medical degree following war service as an army captain. He joined the practice of Dr Forbes-Sempill in the old school building at the eastern end of the village into which he moved his young family. He soon became the weel kent figure that his profession warranted as, duffle coated and with medical bag secured to the pillion, he sped through the village on his Vespa scooter, appropriately nicknamed the 'flying bedpan'. Little did he know that his new colleague was soon to make the national headlines.

Known amongst the locals as Dr Sempill, Raymond's new employer had brought to one of the largest practices in the country a deep understanding and appreciation of the uncompromising area and its folk. Having been born and bred at Craigievar Castle, it had not taken her long to earn the enormous respect and loyalty of her patients. As a 15-year-old in 1952, I had come to know Dr Sempill when her rounds occasionally took her to Mayview. A short, stocky figure with round weather-beaten features, sleaked back hair and clad in heavy tweed more suited to a gamekeeper, her appearance was somewhat at odds with what you might have expected a lady doctor to look like. Her cheery Doric accent and un-fussed approach quickly put at ease even the most accomplished local hypochondriacs.

And then, on Friday, 12 September 1952, a headline in Aberdeen's *The Press & Journal* calmly stated 'Dr Forbes-Sempill Changes Name'.

Dr Forbes-Sempill Changes Name

Dr E. Forbes-Sempill, Brux Lodge, Alford, listed in the Peerage as The Hon. Elizabeth Forbes-Sempill, second daughter of the 18th Baron Sempill, announces to-day re-registration of birth and change of Christian name.

A Public Notice in the advertisement columns of to-day's issue of "The Press and Journal" states that henceforth Dr Forbes-Sempill wishes to be known as Dr Ewan Forbes-Sempill.

The necessary legal steps have been taken to give effect to the re-registration. Recently Dr Forbes-Sempill, on application to the Sheriff at Aberdeen, obtained a warrant for birth re-registration.

Dr Ewan Forbes-Sempill, who is forty, is a member of the well-known family of Forbes-Sempill of Craigievar and Fintray, and has been for several years a general practitioner at Alford.

A recent photograph of Dr Forbes-Sempill

COURTESY OF ABERDEEN JOURNALS

❝Dr E. Forbes-Sempill, Brux Lodge, Alford, listed in the Peerage as The Hon. Elizabeth Forbes-Sempill… announces today re-registration of birth and change of Christian name. A Public Notice in the advertisement columns of today's issue of 'The Press and Journal' states that henceforth Dr Forbes-Sempill wishes to be known as Dr Ewan Forbes-Sempill.❞

The story was quickly taken up by the national press whose reporters were despatched hot foot to a place they had never even heard of. One can only speculate on how they coped with early autumn in 1950s Alford, as temperatures began their downward spiral and a dimly lit Main

Street, devoid of Soho-style distractions, forced them back into the smoky confines of the Haughton Arms bar, while outside the villagers closed ranks in defence of their own. Inevitably the press hacks were forced to justify their expense accounts by filing the speculative trash which is so much part of today's media frenzies.

Three days later Dr Ewan declared that 'the only newspaper which had stated the position correctly and with his approval, was *The Press and Journal*'. He went on, 'One Sunday newspaper yesterday said I will soon announce my engagement to an Aberdeen woman. I absolutely deny that there is any truth in this. It is pure fabrication. Rumours of a forthcoming marriage are entirely without foundation.

Warming to the task and doubtless inspired by Richard Hannay of *39 Steps* fame, our loyal P&J reported how Dr Ewan had, 'deplored the unwelcome attentions of representatives of certain London newspapers who had obstructed him in his duties as a doctor, describing how at one period during the weekend, cars had been stopped on bridges on the Strathdon road near Brux Lodge in such a way that his own car would be unable to pass.

'But, with a smile, Dr Ewan told how he had outwitted the reporters and photographers by travelling in a jeep over the hills and moors to his surgery in Alford.'

And finally, just over a month after the story had first appeared, the P&J rounded off its exclusive coverage with pictures and a report of the marriage of Dr Ewan and his housekeeper, Isabella Mitchell. Weel, weel, an' fa wid hae thocht it!

The Press and Journal

No. 30,485   205th Year   MONDAY SEPTEMBER 15 1952   A KEMSLEY NEWSPAPER   2d

ballito **Rhythm**

...ILDREN ESCAPE AS PLANE ...ROCKS SUNDAY SCHOOL

...ts Run from ...rby Church

...ED PETROL ...DANGER

...of Wallington, Surrey, were talking last about the "miracles" which ...y when a twin-engined civil plane ...ay near the crowded church and ...and burst into flames.

Mr Rodney Carne, of Thornton Heath, Middlesex, of the plane, was killed.

...land Rapide, which had taken off from ...el fuel tanks, fell between the Presbyterian free morning service was being held ...school, where over forty children were ...lessons.

...petrol pump at a nearby garage, where ...el tanks held thousands of gallons of ...struck the wall of the church hall where ...

...pilot suffered, and the stored petrol did ...not explode.

Parents at the church service who had children in the Sunday School ran out anxiously but found them safe, although there had been a moment of panic when the building rocked and flames shot up outside the window.

Middle-aged Miss J. Ferguson, the Bible Class superintendent, quickly calmed the children and led them out.

The minister, the Rev Donald MacArthur, ran in, still in his robes. Among the children were two of his own, a son of four and a daughter of seven.

A 'MIRACLE'

Firemen stopped the flames spreading to the church or the garage.

One man, watching the firemen at work, said: "It couldn't happen in 1952, what's this?"

If the plane had gone three yards further it would have ploughed into the church hall and there would have been many deaths.

The cycle the other way and it would have gone through the towering roof of the church, where 250 people were listening to the minister preaching.

If it had crashed ten minutes later people would have been streaming out of the church and children into the Sunday School.

FLAMES

Three yards to the right and nothing could have saved the plane enveloping the broken petrol pump with flames, and perhaps setting off the thousands of gallons of spirit beneath.

If the aircraft had been a few feet lower as it swayed in its downward course it would have struck a block of flats.

Miss Ferguson said later — "I had just finished my Bible class when there came the sound of an aeroplane.

"Then there was a loud crash and the building rocked. I was stunned for a moment and thought the whole building was going to fall about us. Then I looked through the window. There was an instant of panic, and then I said 'Everybody sit down.'"

She led the children out of the building in single file and on to ...

Mr MacArthur said — "I was preaching when the crash occurred. The next step we heard was the sound of children screaming. I left my pulpit and went to the hall and found the children being led out of the room.

...

The Press and Journal *Told the Truth*

Exclusive Statement by Dr Ewan Forbes-Sempill

DR EWAN FORBES-SEMPILL has instructed his law agents to demand that legal action he may take against certain London newspapers for publishing untrue statements concerning himself and his intentions following his decision to change his name.

The statements to which Dr Forbes-Sempill takes such strong exception were not published in "The Press and Journal."

At his home, Brux Lodge, Strathdon, yesterday, Dr Forbes-Sempill declared that the only newspaper which had stated the position correctly and with his approval was "The Press and Journal," in its issue of last Friday.

Dr Ewan went on:

"I wish to commend 'The Press and Journal' for its restrained treatment of the news of my change of name. It published the correct report.

"Reports which have appeared over the week-end in two newspapers have caused the greatest distress. These newspapers publish exclusive interviews with me. I can assure you that the Press Council which is going to be established to investigate cases of intrusion into people's personal affairs is now functioning.

'Pure Fabrication'

One Sunday newspaper said I will soon announce my engagement to an Aberdeen woman. I absolutely deny that there is any truth in this. It is pure fabrication. Rumours of a forthcoming marriage are entirely without foundation.

"It is too much to hope that the statement which I am now making in 'The Press and Journal' will clear away untruths and misunderstandings? It is too much to hope that I will now be left to live my life in my own way and in peace?"

After all, it is not my fault that this has happened.

Dr Ewan Forbes-Sempill described the deliberate attention of representatives of certain London newspapers, who, he claimed, had obstructed him in his duties as a doctor.

He described how at one period during the week-end cars had been stopped on bridges on the Strathdon road near Brux Lodge in such a way that his own car would be unable to pass.

Over Hills in Jeep

With a smile, Dr Ewan told how he had outwitted the reporters and photographers by travelling in a jeep over the hills and moors to his surgery at Alford.

Dr Forbes-Sempill emphasised that from now on he wanted to be styled Dr Ewan Forbes-Sempill.

Between interruptions throughout the story of how he came to choose the name Ewan.

Brux was once the home of the Camerons. The last of the Camerons lived in it was Sir Ewen Cameron. He was slain by his enemies, the Moivats.

According to the tradition, Lady Cameron, offering the estate of Brux and her daughter's hand in marriage to the man who avenged her husband's death. The man who won a bride and Brux was Alastair Cam Forbes, third son of the Baron of the Black Lip. He married Catherine, heiress of Sir Ewen Cameron of Brux, and Drumallachie, in 1509.

"As I read this in the history of Brux I took a liking to the name Ewen. I changed the form to Ewan—it's a nice Highland name."

The Forbes-Sempill became the third laird of Brux, the family's home at present estate from Lord Sempill.

1000 GREET QUEEN AT CHURCH

WITHIN two hours of her return to Balmoral Castle from her visit to the St Leger, the Queen, accompanied by the Duke of Edinburgh, attended morning service in Crathie Church yesterday.

The weather was cloudy but dry, and a crowd of over 1000 lined the avenue leading to the church to greet her Majesty and the Duke.

The Queen was in cape blue, with a diamond brooch at her lapel. The Duke was in Highland dress.

Earlier the Queen Mother and Princess Margaret had arrived at the chapel from Birkhall. The Queen Mother was in blue and Princess Margaret in black and white ...

The service was conducted by the Rev John Lamb, domestic chaplain to the Queen in Scotland. At the end of the service Provost and Mrs Hogg of the Queen Mother and the Duke in the Royal car. The Queen Mother and Lady Margaret waved every piece of furniture at her home recently in ...

...

HE GAVE HER HALF

A PARIS bank cashier, who worked out an equitable division of household property while ...

Deakin Suffering from Phlebitis

Mr Arthur Deakin, general secretary of the Transport and General Workers' Union and a leading figure in the TUC, is ...

MONTGOMERY AND A MEDAL

Field Marshal Viscount Montgomery was yesterday presented by King Paul of Greece with the insignia of the Grand Cross of the Order of George I of the ...

Food Poisoning?

Food people were taken ill in Renfrew at the week-end ...

Big New Coalfield Under Border?

Results of Borings are Awaited

A LARGE coalfield with reserves estimated at 200,000,000 tons may be revealed on the Scottish border at Canonbie, Dumfriesshire, when borings are completed.

Despite the confined extent of the coalfield, geological and historical clues suggest that England, the divisional deputy could carry out the borings.

This is revealed in a letter from the Minister of State, the Earl of Home, to Major Niall Macpherson, M.P. for Dumfriesshire.

The Minister states that the coal is known to be very deep and, for ...

Clean-up in Cairo Soon

EGYPT'S new Government will speed up trials of corrupt old political figures under arrest to clean the political atmosphere as early as possible and launch preparations for clean and honest elections, it was officially stated at Cairo yesterday.

General Neguib's Cabinet has approved a decree setting up special tribunals for the 1950 ...

CEYLON MISSION OFF TO PEKIN

A Ceylon Commercial Mission to Communist China left here yesterday by air for Pekin to negotiate the sale of rubber ...

U.S. Oil Expert Leaves Persia

Mr Alton Jones, the American oil millionaire who has been advising on the Persian oil question, left Teheran for the U.S. yesterday.

He said he might return to Persia in a month or so to resume his investigations ...

Queen Mother to Tour Refinery

The Queen Mother will visit Grangemouth next Wednesday ...

FIRE AT PAISLEY CHILDREN'S HOME

When fire broke out at Woodside Homes Paisley—a children's home run by the Corporation—early yesterday ...

Jap General Gets Back His Sword

LT.-GENERAL Sir Frederick J. Browning, Household Comptroller to the Duke of Edinburgh, has given back to a Japanese general, a sword which he received from a Japanese commander at the surrender of the Japanese armies in Indo-China seven years ago.

Former Lt.-General Takane ...

Numata wept when he received the sword from Sir Frederick at London, Mr Kenneth Spears now playing Japan with an Oxford University rugby team.

General Browning presented the sword on behalf of the late Lord Mountbatten, Supreme Commander of the Allied Forces in South-east Asia, who received it from the Japanese at the surrender of the Japanese forces in Indo-China.

General Takane, the Japanese Southern ...

from Buckingham Palace and boards are now discussing who should carry out the borings ...

Army presented his sword to Lord Mountbatten at the Twentieth Army Corps headquarters, Saigon.

Sir Frederick felt that Numata's sword should be returned to him after the Japanese peace treaty. Learning that the Oxford team was going to Japan, he asked him to take the sword back.

Monckton Gets Report on Pay Crisis

From Our London Industrial Correspondent

AFTER his return from holiday, the Minister of Labour, Sir Walter Monckton, held a short telephone "conference" yesterday with his Parliamentary Secretary, Mr Harold Watkinson, and his chief industrial commissioner, Sir Robert Gould, on the engineering wages crisis.

"Peacemaker" Sir Robert meets representatives of the Executive of the Confederation of Shipbuilding and Engineering Unions to-day in an attempt to find a formula to bring the two sides of the industry together for talks on a compromise.

His telegram to the Confederation Executive at York on Thursday inviting the union men to a peace parley, postponed their intention to fix a date for an overtime and piece-work ban affecting some of 1,000,000 engineering workers and threatening fine arms and export programmes.

It is not thought likely that Sir Robert will invite representatives of the employers to be present at to-day's talks. He will see them from the confederation secretary, Mr Gavin Martin, a complete picture of the situation as the union men see it, before attempting to bring the two sides closer together.

THIS BOY TOOK AN EXPRESS

Peter Tugwell, aged three and a half of Vapron Road, Plymouth, is a keen engine spotter.

Allowed outside his garden by himself for the first time on Saturday to play he was disappearing and was later found travelling at about 65 m.p.h., curled up in the corner of a compartment of a non-stop Plymouth to London express.

The third found the child asleep and, as the train crashed through St. David's Station, Exeter, he threw out a message.

At Reading, Peter was given a meal by the police and was sent to a nursery school for the night.

His father, Mr R. J. Tugwell, a garage proprietor, arrived at Reading yesterday. Peter was glad to see him and was quite unconcerned about the excitement he had caused. The policewoman who had been taking care of him ...

Maugham Off for Operation

Somerset Maugham left last night for Paris then to travel to Lausanne to undergo a hernia operation.

But Roger Went by Bus

...Roger Parsons ... young bus ... Sheffield ...

Mayor Churchill

Mr Churchill has been made honorary mayor of the small community of Copt-Ael, in the Alpes Maritimes, where the Premier is staying at Lord Beaverbrook's villa.

Mr and Mrs Churchill dined at the casino on Saturday night. Their appearance put an end to rumours that he had remained on the Continent because of illness and was travelling to Australia to see the races. Mme Ballo ...

LATE NEWS

DOCTOR FOUND DEAD

Aberdeen Graduate

Dr George Marsh Glen (47) was found to be lying dead on the floor of his experimental room in Battersea yesterday ...

BRIGHT PERIODS

... Scotland, Orkney and Shetland ... Wind ... north to north-west, light or moderate ... cooler but some bright periods, mist developing ...

Lighting-up Time

Begins, 8.28 p.m. Ends, 5.56 a.m.

U.S. Orders Russians to Quit Frankfurt

AMERICAN Army authorities in Heidelberg yesterday asked the Soviet Commander-in-Chief in East Germany to withdraw the accreditation of three members of the Soviet military liaison mission in Frankfurt.

The members are Lt.-Col Ivan Kaydalov, Capt. Nikolai Dvoichenko ...

BERLIN FACES NEW THREAT OF HUNGER

From Our Own Correspondent

BERLIN, Sunday.—Living in the Soviet zone of ...

In 1984 Ewan Forbes published his memoirs in *The Aul' Days*. The following anecdotes not only give a wonderfully contemporary account of his experiences as a country practitioner, but also record practices which have long disappeared under what many see as the faceless bureaucracy of the NHS.

Country Practice

66 Called out to deal with a child's sore throat, Dr Ewan was greeted by the mother with 'It's Alickie, doctor, he was an awfu' bad birth an' he's never come tae richt'. Suddenly during the examination there was the sound of wood being shattered and a beautiful curved horn emerged through one of the panels. The housewife exclaimed, 'It's the tame lambie doctor'. Asking where she wanted it to go, Dr Ewan pushed back the magnificent horn, applied his knee to its tail end and steered it by its handle-bars into the shed, reflecting that it might have been the 'tame lambie' once upon a time, but long since had become a handsome adult. 99

An Unexpected Confinement

66 One night in Cushnie, after having attended a patient with a heart attack, Dr Ewan was asked to go up to a remote croft where he was told 'There's a wummun arrived here the day an' I'm sure she's gaun tae hae a bairn the nicht'. By the time he had returned with the district nurse and maternity gear, the baby had arrived.

Returning next morning to check the progress of mother and child, he was told that the patient had refused to feed or have anything to do with her baby. In forceful tones the crofter's wife explained how she had handled the situation. 'I said, this is your bairn an' ye're gaun tae feed it. I took the whisky bottle an' rubbit her breists wi' spirit, syne rubbin' the bairn's moo an' pit it tae – it took a guid haud, an' sookit fine. I bad wi' her tae mak' siccar that she did the job richt!'

Later, on discovering that the young mother had gallstones, Dr Ewan had her successfully operated on. Following the operation she was given a jar with all the gallstones in it, and announced with much pride, 'Ye ken there wis abeen a hundred'. 99

Dr Ewan's dedication is summed up in his own words:

Confinements in a Blizzard

66 I vowed that I would never fail to try to get through to any call and kept my vow. I had an old Dodge car like a battleship, and when she had gone as far as she could, my motivation was on skis or snow shoes, or a borrowed Clydesdale, or whiles in great luxury being driven in some kind fairmer's muck sledge with the bottom comfortably filled with straw. This was very convenient for carrying extra gear, like the maternity bag. 99

Bobby

The other keeper of the less savoury secrets of the local populace was Alford's one and only bobby, the lang, lean Hielan' chiel, Lachie Stewart. In a village where 'crime' might amount to local loons chopping down a plantation tree for Christmas, or poaching a salmon from the Don and smuggling it back to the village under cover of darkness, Lachie's commitment to his role must have been sorely stretched, though it has to be said that he blew any chance of promotion through failing to uncover a drinking and gambling ring right under his nose.

Only now can the facts of the case be revealed. How a local Savings Bank manager, doctor and hotelier were engaged in the nefarious pursuit of drinking after hours while playing bridge at a secret location deep in nearby Haughton woods. In truth Norrie, Raymond Hilton and Haughton Arms Hotel proprietor Charlie Spence gathered weekly at Haughton House to indulge in their shared passion for bridge and the delight of the odd dram. Alive to the risk of Lachie Stewart's imminent arrival after

10 o'clock closing time, they kept an eye on the television screen. As Lachie's patrol banger coughed its way closer to the House, horizontal interference on the picture proclaimed that the enemy had been detected. The incriminating evidence having been swiftly removed by the time the law arrived, Lachie was once more left to ponder on the meaning of life within the Aberdeen-shire Constabulary.

Fire!

One other organisation existed to safeguard the local populace and that was the Alford fire brigade, with Leading Fireman Alex (Pa) Gray and firemen 'Jiner' Murray, Jock Milne, Davee Leys and Francee Gilbert ready to sally forth at the drop of a helmet. While no one would deny the significance of the other three organisations, this dedicated band of volunteer firemen stole the show when it came to spectacle.

The sound of the air raid siren above the fire station was the signal for everyone to stop whatever they were doing (although there may have been the odd exception when this might have proved awkward) and race to the station in time to see the arrival of the glamorous crew. Throwing themselves off their bikes or out of their cars, diving into their tunics and donning their striking helmets, they were the envy of every loon in the village. And then the pump engine roared into life, the bell clanged and they were off, leaving in their wake an empty station, carelessly discarded bikes and cars and a babbling bunch of awestruck youth.

Until that is, when the conflagration occurred not only in the village itself, but at the premises of Aberdeen Savings Bank no less. Perhaps a chimney fire hardly merits the term conflagration, but at the time, with sparks flying out into the night sky and two brothers gesticulating wildly behind an upstairs bedroom window, who was I to doubt they were in imminent peril as Alford's plucky firemen launched themselves out of the engine and into the house. Earlier, our gang of loons had abandoned their fish and chips to congeal in Meldie's shack as they hurtled down Greystone Road at the siren's blare and joined the throng outside the station, demanding to know where the fire was.

On being told by one of the crew that it was Mayview, the initial reaction was to deplore the informant's sense of humour, until the engine screeched out and swung into Main Street and all hell broke loose as the village poured after it. As heavily booted firemen crashed through the house with a disappointingly small hose and stirrup pump to extinguish a disappointingly small fire, I was overcome with a bitter sense of anticlimax. I realised any heroic thoughts I had entertained of rescuing my brothers from a fiery fate were dashed by the laughter of the populace as they enjoyed the thespian contortions of Rory and Ian at the upstairs bedroom windows.

Many are the tales of Alford's redoubtable firemen, amongst them the time when, after having dealt with a small outbreak near Tough, at the derelict dwelling of local eccentric 'Black Ackie' Dawson, crew members discovered human excrement in a fireplace – no doubt the unfortunate result of the owner's

Fire! 77

shock induced by the fire, or maybe just a coarse rumour about a coarse chiel. Another involved a wine-tasting spree after they had attended a fire at an aristocratic residence on upper Donside, when a number of bottles from the cellar were 'found' in the back of the fire engine on its return to the station. Lack of a corkscrew necessitated the use of various items of fire-fighting equipment to open the bottles and eventually the crew were able to explore the delights of the grape as opposed to the barley.

Then there was the occasion when there was a call to attend a fire of rucks at Upper Balfour farm. By the time the engine got there the farmer, Victor Davidson, had succeeded in dousing the flames with a farm hose. As the engine slid to a halt, Leading Fireman Gray leapt down from the cab and greeted the farmer with a withering look and the words, 'Aw, Christ, Victor, ye hivna' let it oot, min!'.

The gaunt walls of the Brig shop at the Bridge of Alford still stand as testament to a fire-ravaged grocer's premises which have never been rebuilt following rumours of an insurance scam by the owner, local lad o' pairts Ian Phillips, paramour of the ravishing Isobel and friends of Norrie and Alice. Ian was one of three brothers from one of Aberdeen's big fish merchant families.

The word was, that following a brief journalistic career on the P&J, his father had set him up in the grocery business and next door villa at the Brig. Good looking, entrepreneurial and always seeking outlets for his restless energy, Ian was never destined to become a country grocer, nor the glamorous Isobel a country grocer's wife. From the ashes of the Brig shop then,

Ian and Isobel eventually went their separate ways and Ian took up a teaching career in Aberdeen, where his former pupils are sure to remember him.

Railway

L ike so many other places, Alford owed its initial growth to the arrival of the railway in the second half of the 19th century, so that when rail gave way to road transport in the late 1960s, the village seemed to fall into a decline. Certainly I can remember coming back from time to time during this period and feeling that all that was missing from a rather desolate Main Street was the occasional ball of tumbleweed. But maybe I'd been away too long in more populaced environs.

Since then, thanks to initiatives like Haughton caravan park, Grampian Transport Museum and the Mart Heritage Centre, not to mention a burgeoning commuter population which ironically would welcome the railway's return, Alford has more than recovered its identity.

Back in the Fifties, though, Alford Station exerted a magnetic attraction on a 14-year-old who was mad about trains. Though a far cry from Aberdeen's 'Jynt' Station, end of the line for the big expresses from the south, our end-of-the-line station had its own unique attraction. Located in the village proper as opposed

A goods engine arriving Alford station

to other country stations often found miles from their named destinations, Alford station was an integral part of the community it was built to serve. Perhaps because the LNER seemed a distant, faceless employer for the few local railway employees, the station preserved an aura which stretched back down the line to the outer world and its infinite destinations. From its heyday, fireman Jim Black, goods clerkess Margaret Ingram and porter and signalman Charlie Monk gave a graphic description of the station's importance within the local economy.

Jim Black

❝I arrived at Alford in April 1945 and was a fireman for over three years. Whilst at Alford my driver for most of the time was James Tocher senior who was there for more than 20 years. The guard for our train was usually Alfie Moir who did the shunting along the line although since there was a permanent shunter at Kintore, Alfie was able to take his 'piece' there.

At Alford engine shed there was a a wagon of coal alongside the loco tender, and up to one ton of coal, which should last two round trips, was hand shovelled from one to the other with the help of the shed labourer, Jimmy Anderson.

Jimmy was on from 9pm until to 6am and the train crew started at 5am. If we slept in, Jimmy was there hammering on our doors. After coaling and filling the water tank we did our various oiling jobs. The small fire which was kept up during the night was spread and steam started to be raised. By 6.30am the engine had to be ready to take out the first train leaving at about 7am. We had about 15 regular passengers from Alford, but at Kemnay the train became really busy since a lot of workers from Inverurie Works joined. After leaving the carriages at Kintore we went to the yard, turned the engine and took two carriages back to Alford. We then turned the engine again, easy if it was properly balanced on the table, before returning with the second train to Kintore. By the time we arrived the daily freight would be ready and waiting for us. After a short break we made sure the wagons had been sorted into the correct order for the various stations.

On the way back Alfie would do the necessary shunting and when we eventually arrived back home we coupled off, turned the engine

Alford goods engine at turntable

Loco and shunters at Alford early 1950s

and booked off duty. The late shift re-coaled the engine, refilled the
water tank and worked the goods and passenger trains until night-time
when Jimmy Anderson arrived to clean the engine – and so the time
went pleasantly on!

The main problem from a fireman's point of view was in the Up
direction when the severe climb from Whitehouse meant you had to
have a good head of steam when leaving there and then keep shovelling
all the way to the top. After that the engine did not need much more
than a few shovelfuls leaving the stations as it was downhill all the way
to Kintore. Going home needed gentle firing as far as the summit after
which we could put our feet up.

Coal and its quality led to either good, reasonable or terrible
running. Running badly late meant a report and an Inspector called.
One time Inspector Ramsay got several of these which we said were
due to poor coal, but he did not believe us and duly turned up at
Kintore. He insisted on firing the engine himself to prove it was the

Railway

man not the coal that was at fault. I will just say that on the long, but gentle climb to Tillyfourie his bowler hat was quickly off as were most of his clothes, due of course to bad coal and not bad firing. 99

Margaret Ingram

66 I got a job at Alford just after the passenger trains finished and was responsible for the collection and delivery of goods and all the paper work entailed in that. There were two lorries available all the year round driven by Dod Ellis and Harry Laird. We covered not only the Alford area but also down to Monymusk and up to Strathdon, even on occasion over into Deeside. When things became really busy extra lorries were sent out from Aberdeen. This meant we had to be very careful in giving directions since these drivers did not know the district.

Being a farming area much of the traffic was agricultural. Fertiliser came in on the train and had to be sorted, tallied and sent out on the lorries as quickly as possible. During harvest time we were particularly busy and one of the main things at this time was potatoes.

At really busy times things could, and sometimes did go wrong! This meant that I had to deal with claims for lost or wrongly delivered goods. I remember that several vans of potatoes left Alford, but on their way south one van went missing. The farmer whose tatties they were phoned to say he had not been paid on arrival as promised. It took a lot of telephoning to find that the van had been wrongly shunted somewhere and was over 100 miles from where it should have been. This kind of thing meant a lot of paper work but this was part and parcel of the day's work. And there was not the frantic chase that there is today to get things done immediately. 99

Charlie Monk

66 During the time I was on the railway perhaps the busiest time was between 1955 and 1957 before everybody had, or wanted, a car and the

Alford station staff 1948

freight train carried most things. In the mid fifties at Alford we had two railway lorries on the go from morning till night throughout the year. On top of that there were certain times of the year when we had six or eight extra lorries. When potatoes were going out of the area hundreds of tons could be handled in a season.

Another large seasonal trade was fertiliser and 200 tons or more could turn up and all this had to be manhandled by myself and the two lorry drivers. It took days to deliver to all the farms around and the paper work had to be spot-on. There was a great deal of coal to be off-loaded from the wagons quickly as extra charges became due if they were not emptied and returned right away. Jock Grant dealt with the coal, a big strong lad who shovelled and bagged it all by hand.

During the shearing season farmers had to move their bales of wool from farm to factory and we had to work fast to get this valuable raw material out of the area. You never knew just how many farmers were going to phone daily demanding we collect their wool right away.

Cattle and sheep and the weekly marts provided different problems.

Railway

It was common for them to be brought to the mart at Alford, sold and then walked to the station goods yard where cattle wagons were waiting. Amongst all my other jobs I helped load these wagons and it was often dark when they were eventually ready to go. Lamb sales in particular were hard work at the time but looking back some fifty years later it was all in a normal day's work to us. I also remember at one stage eggs were also sent to Aberdeen by rail. They had to be specially packed in case of shunting accidents, they were messy to clear up!"

At the time, though, all I could think about was waiting on the platform for the arrival of the last train of the day. From the heady moments of its distant whistle, the smoke drifting over the trees and the steadily increasing sound of its clanking approach, I quivered with the anticipation of being allowed to clamber up on to the footplate and drive the engine on to the turntable before running it down to the engine shed for the night. In an age when permitting a youngster to drive a locomotive over an operational line would incur instant dismissal for breaking every health and safety rule in the book, engine driver Alex Birnie, of warm and happy memory, threw caution to the winds and indulged a small boy in an adventure beyond comparison. On reflection, the fact that he shared Norrie's left wing views and was a valued Savings Bank depositor may also have had something to do with it.

A less happy memory was the only journey I ever made on the train from Alford to Aberdeen. A rare and special treat turned into a disaster when I dropped my newly purchased ticket down the inside of the carriage door while letting down the window with the leather strap. Having patiently explained the

Alford train at Kintore 1949

situation to an impassive booking clerk, Norrie was forced to purchase another ticket, a particularly sad reflection on times before 'customer relations' became the buzz phrase.

Kemnay, Monymusk, Tillyfourie, Whitehouse – the station names on the little branch line from Kintore still evoke nostalgic memories. At the time of writing the re-opening of Kintore is very much in the news, so fit aboot an Alford train?

Community

Dirl gings the stairter,
Putter gings the car,
We're awa' for a run
But maybe, no for far.

Maybe up tae Jennie Singer's
For we hear she's no been well
An' fit's adee wi' Jean, we'd like
Tae learn frae Jean hersel'.

Or doon intil the village
Tae news wi' Meg an' John:
Syne further up the glen tae see
Foo Angie's gettin' on.

An' syne, there's Willie's Annie
Fa's partial tae a dram.
Puir wee Annie,
She's awfu' like her mam.

But she winna seek the bottle
Fan we are there tae chat.
Aye, we aft cry in-by Annie's
An' juist because o' that.

Mair fairm machines maks deat
 o' freens
An' sae ye maun agree:
Despite the price o' petrol,
Fa's left, we hae tae see.

For country folk, though scatter
Aye think like neighbours still.
Unless we keep in touch, ye ken
We'll a' gang ower the hill!

Community

Beyond these institutions central to the wellbeing of the village and the surrounding parishes was a vibrant community which knew everything, and more, about its folk and their doings. Gossip, the lifeblood of any village, circulated remorselessly within the heartbeat of homes, shops, clubs and societies which kept Alford alive and well.

SWRI choir

Top of the list of village activities was amateur drama and it was in this world of make-believe that Norrie and Alice saw themselves as missionaries, bringing the wonders of live theatre to the good folk of Alford. But haud on, the Alford Players were in no way ready to accept a couple of 'luvvies' from Aiberdeen who thought they could show these experienced Doric thespians foo tae perform on a stage. It's all there in *Press & Journal* feature writer Norman Harper's evocative piece, 'The Life and Times of the Alford Players'.

66 New Year's night in the Alford of the 1930s, 1940s and 1950s was unnerving for any chance visitor to the village.

Snow fell steadily, softly, on streets strangely silent. Homes were dark, quiet. Narrow lanes and closes were empty. The snow lay deep in the howe. The village appeared deserted; and eerie with it.

Stillness was a commodity in short supply at the village hall, though. There, the only hush came between peals of laughter. The place would have given Tam o' Shanter's auld Kirk at Alloway a run for its money. The Alford Players had taken to the stage again, premiering their latest production. And no one in the howe wanted to miss it.

The seating had been booked solid for weeks. Vitie in the baker's shop had been kept busy taking bookings at 2/6 a time (programme 3d). They were standing in the aisles and round the back of the hall. Children sat two or three deep in the window recesses. The place was packed. And everybody loved every minute of it.

For the brains behind the outfit, postie Bill Marnoch, it was another success. Bill had taken over the old Alford WRI drama group in 1938. By the time he bowed out in 1953, for health reasons, Alford Players' productions were the highlight of the year for many West Aberdeenshire communities.

They rehearsed a production each year from September to

Alford Players

December. It was premiered in Alford Public Hall on January 1, then, for the following 13 Fridays, the Players went on tour. Towards the end, the Players had to ration their performances. Towns and villages were clamouring for a play. It was all they could do to keep their regular customers happy – Ballater, Inverurie, Auchterless, Towie, Lumsden, Dunecht, Torphins, Kemnay and others.

'We must have been good,' said Bill, 'they usually speirt us back.'

Bill was responsible for direction, production, set design, dialogue coaching… the lot.

'I remember Alec Gray and Mackenzie the banker were in a Travers farce,' he said. They were in a double bed and Charlie Grant was hiding underneath. Charlie took a cue and got from under the bed and suddenly the bed collapsed.

Everybody was saying: 'Oh me! What good! How did they manage to time the bed to fa' doon like 'at? In the bed Mackenzie was muttering: 'How the hell do we get out of this, Alec?' And Alec was laughing under the sheets.

'They carried on as though the bed collapsing was just part of the play and the audience lapped it up.'

That was not the only hair-raising moment. Once, the Players were heading back by bus from a show at Kemnay.

'The weather had been bad all day,' said Bill. 'Blizzards were blowing outside all through the performance. We rushed through the play and set off for Alford almost as soon as the curtain closed.

'You could hardly see your hand in front of your face. Well, we got about four miles out the road and we stuck underneath the old railway bridge at Monymusk. Well, that was it. Some of the lads thought they would go outside to see if they could dig us out. They disappeared into this storm.

'Five minutes later, with everybody shivering, there was a knock on the bus door. Alec Gray appeared. ''Scuse me,' he said, 'Zis i' bus for i' Beach?'

It was not all laughs, though. The Alford Players could take their art seriously. Seriously enough to make the divisional finals of the Scottish Community Drama Association one-act play competition one year...

Aileen Murray... remembers playing saucy French maid Yvonne Duchesne in *Money by Wire:* 'I was supposed to get a sexy French wiggle in my walk,' she said, 'but I couldn't make it saucy enough for Mr Marnoch. Eventually, he had to get up on stage to give me a demonstration wiggle. We collapsed laughing.'

Not everyone found the Alford Players so amusing. The hallkeeper at Dunecht refused to allow them to hammer nails into the woodwork to put up their sets.

'There was no way round it,' said Bill, 'We were well and truly stuck. He wouldn't budge. And without the nails we couldn't put on the play. Then someone offered him a dram. He liked it so much he had another. And another. And another... Eventually he was flying around like glory knocking in six-inch nails all over the place. What a grand chap he was every year after that.

But perhaps the best story concerns a production at Inverurie Town

Alford SWRI choir

Hall. One actor had a walk-on part at the end of the play. He had to portray a tipsy gent who walked on with a parcel and walked off.

During the first part of the play he was nowhere to be seen, but, reliable soul that he was, his fellow actors were unconcerned. He would turn up. Sure enough, minutes before he was due to walk on, he turned up, collected his parcel, staggered on stage, said his piece and staggered off.

The Inverurie audience were spellbound by this cameo of an inebriate. 'At boy should be in i' fillims,' they said, 'that's a right good actor, 'at. Michty, ye'd think he wis really pi… really pittin' his hert and soul intil't' Backstage, the stage hands were having a hard time calming the frantic actor. 'Far's the parcel,' he was saying, 'I'm on in a few min'ties.'

'He'd forgotten he'd just been on,' said Bill. 'In fact he'd probably forgotten he'd been up at the Butcher's Arms for some time before he went on stage. He was bleezin' something rotten. But Inverurie thought he was a first class character actor.'

Every one of the Alford Players has fond stories to tell of their acting days. All say it was hard work, but enjoyable work. They would not have missed it for the world.

And doubtless the memories linger on with thousands of West Aberdeenshire people who flocked to their village halls for an evening of real family entertainment in pre-TV days.

Norman Harper concluded his feature:

> I sorely regretted having missed being part of something which gave such a strong sense of teamwork to the people of a small Donside village, something which so obviously held a special place in the hearts of Donside and fostered a communal warmth in the wee towns and villages of West Aberdeenshire during those soft, dark, wintry nights 30 or 40 years ago. 99

Finally, my own vivid recollection is of Jock Stewart in full and magnificent Highland dress, stepping down from a huge framed 'portrait' in the Players' acclaimed production of *The Bonesetter*. Jock

Aberdeen County Council—Education Com
Youth and Community Services

Youth Drama Festiva

COUNTY FINA

in

Inverurie Town Hall,

on

FRIDAY, 13th APRIL, 195

at 7.45 p.m.

———

Chairman:
MAITLAND MACKIE, Esq.,
Chairman, Aberdeenshire Education Comn

Adjudicator:
JOHN F. GROVES, Esq.,
Director of Technical Studies,
Scottish College of Drama.

Stage Director:
GEORGE SCOTT, Esq.
Inverurie.

Programme Price Sixpence.

had sat absolutely motionless throughout an act before emerging from the 'portrait' to the accompaniment of realistic thunder and lightning effects. An audible gasp of genuine shock went through the captivated audience as the ghost of the clan chief emerged on to the darkened stage. National Theatre, eat your heart out!

Norrie felt that audiences might welcome the opportunity to turn up at the village hall more than once a year to sample a more varied diet of theatrical offerings. Accordingly, he not only launched the Alford Community Club but under its auspices also applied for Arts Council subsidies to bring professional dance, music and theatre companies to the village. Soon the Club was entering productions for the Scottish Community Drama Association's One Act Play Festivals and

---

ALFORD COMMUNITY CLUB

DESPERADO"

by Leonard D. Francquhem

rs	Players
n innkeeper	Brian McEwan
his wife	Helen Simpson
old woman	Freda Brown
a young man	William Chapman
a priest	William McKenzie
lawyer	Lawrence Johnstone
his son	Leslie Murray
daughter of Zina	Rhona McCarthy
wife of Dineppo	Susan Hilton
a brigand	John Begg
a brigand	John McCombie
a brigand	Callum McKenzie
, chief of the brigands	Rory McEwan

A street in a lonely mountain village called Minadua, in a country (imaginary) where, and at a time, when brigands terrorised the inhabitants of such villages.

Producer: Norman McEwan

Stage Manager: W. Marnoch

Alford Community Club winners of County Youth Drama Festival in 1956.

giving local youth their first ever opportunity to 'tread the boards' in the County Council's Annual Youth Drama Festival, which they won on both the occasions they entered.

By this time Norrie had teamed up with Alford Players supremo, Willie Marnoch, and together they devised and directed the Alford entry in the Top Town competition where they blew the opposition away at the finals in Inverurie. Top Town took its inspiration from the BBC TV series at the time, showcasing the talent of village and town entrants across the county. Within the Alford contingent, hairdresser Jimmy Ingles demonstrated his magician skills under the billing of 'Sleeko Jeemy Inglee'. The show finished with an epilogue written by Norrie and delivered by the stage manager.

There's No Business Like Show Business

There's just a minute left to our finale,
In fact, they're really ready for it now:
When we'll sing the final chorus
Like Kemnay did before us
And smile and wave our hands and
take a bow.

And so, our little show will then
        be over,
And our producer's nerves be quiet
        at last:
He's done his best to coax our laughter
And whatever happens after
His troubles, poor old fellow, will
        be past.

He really didn't want a poem at
        this point,
'A comedian', he said, 'right here
        would just be great':
But to be a solo comic
Takes conceit, or talent astronomic
And we're happier, and safer,
        playing straight.

But though we're happier and safer
        playing humble,
Make no mistake, we're glad we
        played tonight:
For with television such a catch
We can't all sit and watch
Local effort slowly die without a fight.

And there's one thing must be said
        before we finish,
And this applies to Inverurie, Keith,
Kemnay, Alford and all the rest:
A good design for living must include
        the art of giving
And every team has surely given of
        its best.

97

Entertainment

In the meantime Norrie had decided to work towards an Associate of the Drama Board (ADB) qualification and having achieved this, professionally adjudicated drama festivals around the county and beyond. On these occasions I often accompanied him, enjoying the performances while learning the elements of acting and direction at first hand, though these were initially confined to puppet shows in the old tailor's workshop at the back of the house. Here our little company performed weekend shows on a makeshift stage with home-made marionettes, stage lighting and musical accompaniment from an old wind up gramophone, to full houses of the village loons and quines who were charged a penny for the privilege.

But ultimately it was the celluloid world of the picters which seduced young and old alike in the Glen Cinema's Saturday night monochrome screenings in the village hall. Even then it took a pretty powerful storyline to hold the attention of a youthful audience, already restive on the backless wooden benches which comprised the 'front stalls'. The backed benches

Village Hall

occupied by older members of the audience were little better, though during a particularly demanding film they prevented the more senior citizens from falling backwards in their somnolent state.

On such occasions the loons and quines found happy distraction in smashing bars of 'coo candy' on the benches and pelting Bill Smith the hall keeper with sweeties, while he raged back and forth in the darkness, waving the pencil glare of his torch ineffectually at his tormentors.

Galloping down Kingsford Road in thigh-slapping mode following a Western was nothing compared to our reaction after viewing *The Long and the Short and the Tall,* a war film in which our brave soldiery took on the 'yellow peril' in the jungles of east Asia. Captivated by the voices of the enemy emerging from the surrounding darkness of the jungle, 'Bleeteesh Johnnie, we you come to get,' as they waged psychological warfare on the heroic British squaddies, we adopted a whole new language and inflection in our day to day communication thereafter.

From the Alford Players' launch of the New Year, the village hall, hub of the community, hosted a programme of events throughout the year. Socials, dinners, dances, fund-raising occasions, club activities – all combined to keep the community alive and well and as far as nascent youth was concerned, none more so than the dances. Now was the chance to put into practice the lessons learned in the gymnasia of Inverurie Academy, though first you had to overcome the trauma of crossing the floor towards the ranks of local quines, all affecting disinterest. And when, after an age, you confronted the object of your desire and blurted out, 'May I have the pleasure', only to be refused, you wanted the earth to swallow you up as you desperately searched for an alternative partner, only to find they had all been snapped

Corrennie Dance Band

Alford lasses at Public Hall dance

up. If that was bad, the ladies' choice was even worse, when the one you'd eyed up all evening chose some second rate, acne-ridden partner and you found yourself faced by an acutely unattractive quine you'd been avoiding all evening. Perhaps it was time to go home, squeeze your plukes again in front of the mirror and apply another swab of stinging surgical spirit.

But sometimes it all went right and as the fiddle, concertina, saxophone and piano of the Corrennie Dance Band gently blended into the last waltz under the slowly revolving crystal ball, dappling its colours across the hall, she'd let you pull her close until your cheeks touched and you knew you would be walking her home and into uncharted territory.

Seasons

While characters and events create the detail on the canvas of our memories, the overarching background must surely be the seasons, without which village life would be directionless. So with Alford, where each of the seasons played its time-honoured role in determining the way the people of the parish lived, worked and finally returned to the land from whence they came.

Throughout the year, the seasons were reflected in the Tuesday mart when the farming community and their beasts arrived in force and the village geared itself up for the fray. Floats loaded with bellowing cattle and bleating sheep frae a' the airts funnelled into Main Street where they took their chance amongst the mayhem of drovers' oaths and animals being driven down the sharn -splattered roadway. The unpredictability of livestock on the hoof increased when the terrified craiturs reacted to the beatings of the drovers, veering off right and left as they stampeded up side lanes and into the back gardens of houses bordering the main thoroughfare. In this respect Mayview was particularly

Alford Heritage Centre

well placed and Norrie's carefully managed celery trenches took on the forlorn aspect of a shell-pocked no man's land.

When mart days coincided with school holidays, it was a delight to ride in the cab of Sandy Hosie's float. This highly contested privilege was gained by getting down to the mart at the crack of dawn, before any other youthful competitor, and helping to unload the first cargo of the day. That achieved, you climbed aboard, affecting not to make eye contact with disconsolate rivals as you inwardly celebrated your triumph. Then we trundled up farm tracks and into the farmyards, driving the beasts up and down the slippery ramp and revelling in the responsibility of mind over splatter. At the end of mart days, Sandy would unhitch his float and for the rest of the week revert to the role of general haulier between Aberdeen and the Howe, carrying anything and everything that would fit on the lorry. Pressed into service for furniture removal, the float provided yet another source of income for the enterprising Sandy whose vehicle must have repaid its original investment many times over. Sandy's transport activities presented yet another challenge to those beefy youngsters seeking driver's mate status. This involved walking away from the village towards Aberdeen in the hope that you would be the first to flag him down and climb aboard for the rest of the day. The reward of sailing past those who faced a long and pointless trek back was icing on the cake.

The mart stood at the end of our back garden, separated by a track which led to the livestock pens; the spectacle of the animals as they galloped past was like sitting on the edge of a Wild West stampede. Later when the day's sales commenced, we sat on the tiered wooden platforms surrounding the ring in which the beasts were paraded in twos and threes. The auctioneer's incomprehensible quick fire babble responded to the farmers whose bids only he could identify by the surreptitious lift of an eyebrow, stroke of a chin or other apparently meaningless gesture of which the ordinary spectator was totally unaware. Beyond the ring, ranged along a wide corridor, were the offices of the agricultural sales and insurance representatives ready to do business with their farming clients, while the women folk, revelling in their once-a-week release from the labours of the farm, patronised the shops.

Later the aroma of mince and tatties pervaded the building as lunch was prepared. At other times the mart was the venue for

Alford Museum

roups, when the village gathered to view and bid for the worldly possessions of a family whose property had been sold, their belongings unceremoniously piled up in the auction ring.

Elsewhere, excitement and daring went hand in hand during the annual raids on the 'craw woodie'. Just off the Keig road on the edge of Crookmore Farm, platforms of branches atop a ragged group of pines housed, at dizzying heights, the broad nests of twigs on which clutches of crows' eggs lay ripe for daylight robbery. Defying vertigo, loons shinned up the long trunks until they emerged in the topmost branches and set to work while the demented parents circled above cawing their despair. Eggs were dropped from a great height and caught in caps, except when bursts of raucous laughter signalled direct hits on those whose judgement had gone awry. The climax to these activities was especially satisfying as, pockets filled with eggs, the daylight raiders hurtled through Montgarrie on their bikes, pelting the windows of shops unfortunate enough to be in the line of fire.

And so ploughing, drilling and seed-time succeeded each other through spring into summer. Flocks of screaming gulls, revelling in their inland diet, hovered and dived behind the tractor as its driver leaned backwards in his bouncing metal seat, looking over his shoulder to check his furrow in the rich, black soil of the Howe. The peewits poked about in the freshly-turned slabs of moist earth while the whole Vale celebrated the glorious contrast of luscious new grass and newly ploughed soil.

Norrie, however, had now been around long enough to know that a North-East spring was merely an unpredictable transition between the extremes of winter and the possibility of something called summer.

As spring gave way to summer, so the thoughts of adolescent loons skewed violently towards the quines, as school gym slips, winter coats and headscarves metamorphosed into thigh revealing tennis skirts, fresh white open-necked blouses and gaily patterned, sleeveless summer dresses.

Our summers were the paltry few weeks of holiday which marked the interval between the end of the academic year and the return to school before autumn had really commenced. With boundless energy and a wild desire to strip off school garb, we headed, native-like, for the towering beeches of Haughton

Spring Cleaning

It's Mairch and pagan Achie gaunts upon his Ben,

Yestreen, he sweepit' a' the howe and hoovered ilka glen,

He nicket the last leaf frae the beech and scrubbed
    the hedgerow bare;

Syne scour't ayont Aquorthies his kirkit stanes wi' care.

Though hine awa' there's nimbus, the lift is blue abune,

Jock daunders up the Davah hill, his fat dog drags ahin'.

Ah weel, through gless it's simmer

But there's aye that bitter win'.

For mercy Achie has nae eese, nor sic like Christian ploys,

A'dwynin life and frail auld fowk are taen like broken toys.

Sae, a' at aince, the lift gangs grey and a blast o' sleety snaw

Shooms whirlin' ower the winnelstrae tae ca' puir Jock awa'.

Rax in yer pooch an' tak that pill o' nitroglycerine,

Gin ye win hame, we'll hae a dram, John Anderson ma frien'.

Syne, never mair get nabbit on the briest o' Davah's brae

Tae strive wi' scaffie Achie on a snell spring day.

Woods and fast-flowing, gurgling waters of the Don, where salmon could be poached in the gloaming and hidden in the woods before their collection after dark.

Younger days were spent climbing and swinging from the huge branches of the Tarzan tree, a massive beech which made an awesome impression even amongst its fellow giants. It was eventually felled during a massive storm. Norrie captured the devastation of the younger populace in a nostalgic article for the Inverurie 'Squeak'.

The Tarzan Tree

❝Country kids are lucky. Adults are tolerant towards them and the very occasional 'clap ower the lug' is only handed out when liberty has become obvious license. Even the local bobby, although firm, is usually merciful.

But country kids have space. Space in which to evade the law. Space in which to grow. Space in which to dream like their fore fathers who dwelt in earth houses and dreamt of better things.

Like these ancients, our children had a rude temple. For generations, this was the established meeting place and centre of their youthful world. It was a tree. Called the 'Tarzan tree' on state occasions, but usually referred to as the 'Tarzaner' by young but blasé habitués. It was an old and huge beech with a multitude of monstrous branches which started spreading low down so that access was as easy and climbing simple as the solid branches above were safe and plentiful. Because we once were, maybe, monkeys, kids love trees. Certainly, primitive man was on occasion, a tree dweller for reasons of security.

For security, too, he often dwelt on islands. Kids love islands. Any accumulation of spate material in the Don, which grows until it breaks surface, becomes a treasure island in the eyes of the young and with reeds, long grasses, and the beginning of a tree or two on top, it is irresistible. It must be conquered, the natives pacified and the entire territory fortified to resist further invasion.

The Tarzaner was different. It was a temple. Rites were practised there. Rites involved daring which would have terrified the gentle makers of adventure playgrounds. But nothing adverse ever happened. The final rite was formal. A test of junior manhood. The boy stood on a huge, horizontal branch about twelve feet above ground. Facing him, at eye level, another branch at a distance very depressing to the chicken mind. He had to gather himself then leap from safety and, as his palms slapped the target, grasp and hang on until his body stopped swinging. Then he could drop to the ground to show his contempt for the height or to demonstrate fatigue or, complete success, work his way back along the branch to the safety of the tree.

The bark on that branch was well worn with success and scratched with failure. There was little danger. Only a complete miss could mean a heavy landing and, as this rite was a final one played only by experienced Tarzans, there were no total misses.

It never rained beneath the Tarzaner. Even without foliage, the broad branches stopped all but a few, clever drips. Its joys lasted until a boy or a girl took their first courting walk and carved their initials on its ample surface. Then the tree meant nothing more to them and the realities of life took over.

The great gale came to Aberdeenshire and blew it down. It cut great swathes through forest and sent new henhouses hurtling while sparing a rickety shed tucked in the lee of some old, cottar house. Being pre-Hydro days the puny power lines of private enterprise collapsed as did the poles and telephone wires of Her Majesty.

Little towns, encompassed by fallen timber, were cut off as the short January daylight ended and country folk prepared for a night of dying storm.

With daybreak, a rude assessment of damage could be made. It was immense. Quickly and without arrangement, the children from all around set out for the Tarzan tree. The woodland had suffered almost total loss. The great and mighty trees had fallen, wrenching up their deep foundations which, now vertical, were walls, as high a houses, built of roots and earth and stone. The children picked their way through devastation to their tree. It was untouched. Only twigs and old wood had been shed to mock the fury of the wind.

A year and a half later, there was another storm which is not recorded in the annals of the parish. Thunder and lightning, alarming at first by reason of proximity. As its rumblings and flashing moved slowly away, the virtuous dropped off to sleep while the sinners slept soundly through it all. Next day, the children came, as usual, in ones and twos and chosen groups to play at the Tarzan tree. There, they gathered slowly in a loose and silent ring. The hands of the young ones sought the reassuring clasp of a big brother or sister and, for once, this boon was not denied. Split from top to bottom, their tree had suffered what we adults call 'an act of God'.

Slowly, the silent ring dissolved. The children went away. By narrow paths through willow herb which filled the clearings. The children went away and never came back. The Tarzaner was dead. 99

Next to the bowling green with which it shared the pavilion that divided them, stood the tennis courts. Perhaps it was Wimbledon fortnight relayed on primitive television screens which caused our gang of four to investigate tennis facilities in the village. Two run-down courts in the Pleasure Park, witness to an earlier era when tennis had been a popular pastime, were all that remained. Surrounded on three sides by a beech hedge and enclosed by worn high fencing, the weed-covered courts, in dire need of re-surfacing, presented a challenge to teenagers on a mission to bring tennis to Alford once more. Under the expert tutelage of Norrie's bridge-playing cronies, Doc Hilton and farmer George Hewitt, both useful English tennis players, we set to work measuring and re-surfacing the courts, repairing the fencing and sprucing up the pavilion.

Soon Alford Lawn Tennis Club was back in business and a force to be reckoned with in the Donside Tennis League. To qualify for selection, the fledgling four had to undergo crash coaching sessions with our elders, one of whom was Norrie, who delighted in standing in the centre of the court, replying to my desperate returns with viciously-angled shots which drove me not only from side to side, but ultimately to distraction. Sadly, however, it was not Norrie on whom I wreaked my revenge but dear old Doc Hilton who, defeated by me in a singles match, ran forward and leapt over the net to congratulate his young opponent. Frozen in time, I still preserve the image of the dear fellow, one moment in mid air as the toe of his tennis shoe just clipped the net cord, the next flat on his face, glasses flying across the court, then leaping to his feet as though nothing untoward had happened to shake my hand. Raymond Hilton, the epitome of an English gentleman.

The ultimate, though rare experience, came after a blistering summer afternoon's manic tennis, leaping on to our bikes, dookers already under our shorts, and belting the mile or so across to Montgarrie where, just below the old Bailey brig, we threw ourselves into the Don and cooled off in the depths of the 'Potty'.

The other Donside League, football, was centred as indeed every sport was, in the Pleasure Park. There on summer evenings Alford Favourites were cheered on by the locals as they did battle against the visiting teams from Lumsden, Rhynie, Keig, Monymusk and Kemnay. We worshipped our local heroes – loppy-lugged goalie Ted Forsyth of the yellow polo-necked sweater; all round athlete and skilled footballer Cyril Mutch; Sandy Beaton of the floppy locks and hair net; glamour boy Bertie Stuart…

Strangely enough for a Scottish village, Alford also boasted a formidable cricket club which, following a fast ball in the nether region, I declined to join.

The big annual summer events were the Alford Show, and Gala Day, when the village was bedecked with patriotic red white and blue bunting and Main Street became awash with youngsters in fancy dress – from Rob Roy to Robin Hood, Florence Nightingale to Mary Queen of Scots – demonstrating an historic and national awareness unrivalled among today's net - surfing generation.

In another of his 'Squeak' contributions, Norrie recalls a particular day of celebration in a particular village.

A Coronation Day Recollection

❝Gala week in Inverurie and, this morning, my neighbour across the street produced bunting to be strung from his window to mine. With my fumbling assistance, it now flutters bravely in the breeze and takes my rambling memory back to Coronation Day.

Then, I knew a little man who lived across the way from someone most important. Coronation Day was soon to come and busy was this village with thoughts of bunting and the like. The little man bought bunting to the best of his resources and assumed that his neighbour

Alford Favourites FC

opposite would act as anchor for his humble show and that, likewise, he would take the strain for the big man's finer flags. As thought the wife and children of the little man too.

Nor did the little man make the first approach. He knew his place. He waited to be told his duties in the matter to comply forthwith. One morning he awoke – wakened by his worried children. Flags had been strung from the big man's house but not his. Angled, they crossed the street from left to right of the little man's abode. Fastened, on the left to the Bank's imposing bulk and, on the right, to the grandeur of the grocer's. His wife was quiet. His children were disconsolate. Worse still, they wished to know the reason.

How could he explain without destroying their faith in man? Worse still, destroying their faith in important men? Sadly, he strung his little lot of unassuming flags across his own house front.

Came Coronation Day. Now although in theory, the village street is accessible to all from everywhere, only local traffic may be expected there. The main road is different and carries the commerce of our country. What happened that morning, happened not before, has not happened since and will not happen in the future.

Coronation Day was cold and wet. The weather made a mockery of June. All down the street, the sodden strings of bunting crossed its length from house to house except that gap before the house front of the little man. There his little Hong Kong flags dismally dripped against the wall. Ten miles a way, there is a turning off the main road which, to a strange driver beset with wind and rain and faulty wipers, might just confuse him for a moment and tempt him from the trunk road. And if his load and vehicle were sufficiently unwieldy, he might have to carry on regardless as turning back could not be done.

So, if you believe in natural causes thus it must have happened. At the entrance to the village, there appeared a huge transporter carrying, of all things, an enormous bomber. Wingless, but with its upper gun turret high above the houses. At a steady 30 mph it slid down the main street sweeping away all preparations for the day. The gun turret's base swathed itself with flags leaving not a scrap of glory to be seen. Except the now triumphant bunting still colouring the house front of the little man.

The driver and his mate were a mile beyond the village before the penny dropped. Back they came, on foot, carrying a tangled, soaking bundle of useless pennants.

Coronation Day continued without them. As the wet, cold day came to a close and the bonfire's embers hissed in the rain, the little man put out the cat and looked at the leaden sky.

Suddenly, there was a clear patch and a single star shone clear. 'Someone up there', he thought, 'has a sense of humour and, maybe, a sense of justice too'. 💬

Top of the season's calendar and highlight of the year was the Vale of Alford Agricultural Show, a veritable showcase of endeavour and achievement which brought together the best in everything our agricultural heritage had to offer. Years may have

Alford cricket club

dimmed the memory, but I can only remember Show days when
the sun blessed the event, a just return for the labours of the
farming community beyond and across the Howe.

An early morning haze hung over the dew soaked show park
on the edge of the village, doon the 'lang stracht' just off the
Montgarrie Road, and the evocative smell of damp hay
permeated the chill air enveloping the early arrivals of livestock
and exhibitors. Under a huge marquee was an assortment of
platforms, trestle tables, benches and bales of straw ready to be
manoeuvred into position for the exhibitors' stalls, bar and dining
areas and a stage which would come into its own later in the
day. As the sun slowly dispersed the mist, the show park revealed
an arena where painstakingly groomed Clydesdales in their
shining harnesses, glowering black Aberdeen Angus beasts,
lowing dairy cattle, upright rams and apprehensive sheep would
shortly be paraded before the critical gaze of the judges,

identified from the hoi polloi by the blue rosettes on the lapels of their heavy tweed jackets. By late morning, the winners stood in their paddocks displaying a colourful array of rosettes, which would join other trophies pinned above stalls in stables and barns. Meanwhile under the spreading folds of the marquee local produce was under the scrutiny of another set of judges as they circulated around the tables laden with baking, from Victoria sponges to bannocks. Fruit, vegetables and flowers completed this cornucopia of country goodness. Soon the aroma of home cooking drifted among the chattering spectators as lunch was prepared and the bar opened for business. Now the sun was in its heaven and as its rays beat down upon the canvas, beads of perspiration appeared on the weather-beaten features of farmers as they sank their pints in celebration or consolation.

Outside, the arena was being prepared for the afternoon's feats of physical strength and agility where local heroes competed with the travelling group of 'professionals' well versed in traditional Highland sports. Chief amongst the professionals was popular local farmer, Henry Gray, a good natured giant of a man and a legend in his time. Good money was to be had across a series of events from tug o' wars and races, to caber and hammer.

Finally another Show drew to a close and as the older folk made their homeward way, the young were gearing up for the marquee dance. The carnival was in full swing and groups of giggling quines in high heels and summer finery tottered around the garishly lit fairground, their shrieks on the dodgems and swing-boats studiously ignored by their male counterparts, seri-

Vale of Alford Show were restricted
here we see some of them "showing
fore the spectators during the parade.

At the Vale of Alford Show

The Vale of Alford Agricultural
Association Show was held in good
weather at Alford on Saturday. Left
—Proud owner, Mr C. A. Coutts,
Greystone, Tullynessle, with the
show champion and her foal.
Below—Ten-year-old Margaret
Black, Tarland, and two-year-old
Ann Mathers, Alford, take part
in the fancy dress parade.

ILLUSTRATION COURTESY OF ABERDEEN JOURNALS

ously involved at the airgun stalls.

The timber flooring was laid out in the marquee, the Slipperine applied and the band on the stage ready to break into waltz, quickstep and foxtrot, interspersed with Gay Gordons, Dashing White Sergeant, Boston Two Steps and Eightsome Reels.

And so 'the minutes wing'd their way wi' pleasure' until all too soon the last waltz signalled the now or never moment to ask whether you could 'tak her hame'. If the answer was yes, a wave of giddiness swept over you and you felt ten feet tall.

Alford summers were marked by the visit of the North-East's very own regiment, the Gordon Highlanders. Led by their braw pipe major, immaculate in their uniforms, they would beat the retreat at the Fountain in the evening, kilts swinging in rhythm, with the skirling of the pipes and the staccato rat-a-tat-tat of the drums raising the hairs on the back of your neck.

It was easy to see how the regiment, 150 years earlier, would have tempted wide-eyed youths away from a life of drudgery and hardship,

> *'... over the mountains and over the Main,*
> *Through tae Gibraltar and France and Spain,*
> *Wi' the feather on yer bonnet and the kilt abune yer knee,*
> *Enlist bonny laddie an' come awa' wi' me'.*

The popular Clayton family of tinkers set up camp each summer at the entrance to the village, in the narrow strip of wood between road and railway. Here, bronzed and weather beaten, dad, mum and kids seemed content with their existence, living under cover in a makeshift hut of canvas and spending their days grinding and sharpening the knives and tools of the villagers. Funnily enough, no-one ever saw them arrive or depart. One day their little encampment was there and the next, gone, with just the cold embers of their cooking fire witness to the little group of wandering souls.

In theory, Coronation Day June 1953 might have been the climactic event of all our Alford summers. Sadly, it didn't live

Norrie and Alice

up to expectation, as Norrie recorded in 'The Big Chute'.

The Big Chute

❝The big chute was the community's gift to the children on
Coronation Day. Coronation Day which dawned so cold and wet and
continued thus until its close. A June day which began with speeches
from the cricket clubhouse veranda by local, little bigwigs to an
audience mainly composed of brownies, guides, cubs and scouts. The
brownies seemed to suffer most from the wind and rain, but all were
wet, cold and miserable. Even the few adults, who bordered these
serried ranks, had re-assumed their wintry, blue and bitten look and
heavy clothes to match the weather. The speeches were too long and
lengthened still by recurrent faults in the aged and hastily erected
public address system. At last, the final platitude had been processed
and the scattered hand-claps of dutiful applause terminated the horror
of another official opening ceremony. It was then, with
unpremeditated cruelty, the children were served with ice-cream
cornets.

The company set off across the park through the wet grass and
driving rain to the big chute. Now that the platform party was also
under the weather, the formalities were modified. The high class lady,
not wasting time, launched herself down the chute only to stick half-
way as her substantial, tweed skirt collected water and brought her to a
soggy halt. Blessed thus by total defeat, the children were herded to the
vast SAI tattie shed where the banker dispensed the Coronation
handouts. The day ended with rain hissing on the bonfire's embers
and puddling the wanton tyre marks across the cricket pitch.

And all this recapitulation caused by a reference to the overgrown
sand-pit. Well, the sand-pit was something. The children used it.
Swings, turntables, see-saws and even big chutes are difficult to add to
by imagination and kids get bored with repetition. So you swing, turn,

see-saw, slide, you still hanker after something more. The ramparted sand-pit was often some kind of fort. Always lightly held and invariably besieged by big battalions with ample divots to provide a dirty barrage before the final charge and slaughter of the defenders. Defenders who died theatrically and with style. Still, who needs a sand-pit? Who needs a play park? Any waste ground with trees and bushes and a burn will do excellently. Perhaps the district council was wise enough when it let the sand-pit go. 99

Our last few days of summer freedom were spent hairsting in the parks of George Hewitt's Mains of Tonley farm, desperately trying to keep up with the binder as it trundled back and forth, throwing out the sheaves which we grabbed two at a time under each arm and thrust into stooks of eight for drying. Then came the leading when the dried sheaves were pitch-forked on to the trailer and brought back to the farmyard for ruck building pending the arrival of the threshing mill and the bagging of another summer's golden crop.

'But pleasures are like poppies spread' and so it was back to another endless academic year of early mornings, long bus journeys and regimented days. Autumn crept in imperceptibly until darker mornings, shorter days and plummeting temperatures registered the irrevocable onset of winter.

The tatties were now ready to be lifted and each weekend the farmers vied to outbid each other with reckless offers ranging from 10/- (50p) to 15/- (75p) for a day's back-breaking toil as they tried to tempt the canny young labour force towards their tattie parks. From seven o'clock on weekend mornings, tractors with straw-lined trailers circled the Fountain as empowered local youth questioned the availability of such perks as the length of piece and lunch breaks, the quality of the food on offer and lousin' time. Tolpuddle Martyrs eat your hearts out. Decisions made, the workers headed to their tattie parks where their labours were described by Norrie in *The Young Tattie Picker*.

By this time the tattie pickin' spoils had added up in the green Aberdeen Savings Bank books and the handwritten entries, carefully dried on the intersecting pages of pink blotting paper, recorded that it was time for Alford loons to hit the toon with their hard won earnings. A crisp ten bob note bought you a glorious day out in the Silver City, including your return bus fare, a morning alternating between the freezing waters and steaming showers of Justice Mill Lane baths, a newspaper wrapped stack of non-Meldie quality fish and chips from the chipper opposite, a Wild West afternoon in the Odeon, Capitol, Majestic or Gaumont, rounded off by coughing your way through a five pack of Woodies in the smoke-wreathed back seat of the homeward bus. Greater than all these put together, however, were the first stirrings of independence from parental authority and financial restraint.

Hairsts and tatties apart, the best earner was grouse beating which started on the 'Glorious Twelfth'. Now this was real man's work, demanding the strength and resilience of athletic youth for a day's slog on the heather-covered slopes and boggy moors of the surrounding estates like Craigievar. Marshalled by the gamies in their tweed suits and deerstalkers, we were driven mercilessly round the flanks and over the tops of hills until we collapsed for a blessed hour to munch our humble fare. We envi-

The Young Tattie Picker

The grievie pairs us aff
An' taks us doon the dreel,
'Noo's the time tae show,' he says,
'Yer smeddum an' yer skeel'.

We are a mixter-maxter lot
O' loons an' quines an' deems.
Wi' skulls tae haun, we staun atween
Oor bitties mark't wi' breems.

Ma neighbour's gey sma' biggit
An' I hope he isnae sweer
But the tractor starts its bummin'
An' yokin' time is here.

Pickin' a crap o' tatties
Turns the frosty grun tae weet
An' sune a muckle crap o' dubs
Is clairtit tae each beet.

The skulls are fill't an' teem't and fill't
An' teem't and fill't aince mair
An' teem't an' fill't an' teem't an' fill't
'Til ilka back is sair.

Fan denner-time has come an' gone,
The efterneen drags on and on:
A lang an' weary trauchle
For aye we're chauvin' on until
Ma spang becomes a shauchle.

The tractor comes at sic a lick,
The howker's fairly fizzin'.
Ah'm shair it's towerin' faister noo,
Aye saxteen tae the dizzen.

But, losh, at last, the howkin's dune
An' the githerin' is here
And, in a line, we a' drag doon
The park tae clean it bare.

Oh, but ma back is yarkin' noo,
The park's grown unco big.
Ah'm shair it wisnae hauf this size
Fan they began tae dig.

The dubs that clairtit a' ma beets
Are ower the tap an' roon ma cuits.
Ah'm runtit fairly wi' the wark
An' soakin' in ma sweaty sark.

It micht help noo if some chiel had
The hert tae sing a sang:
An', oh, ah wish that lousin' time
Winna be ower lang.

ously observed the gentry reaching into their bottomless wicker hampers to reveal exotic culinary delights, champagne corks popping to the accompaniment of overloud guffaws as they celebrated the morning's bag.

On a more nostalgic note, Norrie remembered the rolling slopes of Craigievar which overlooked the Howe.

Fan summer comes tae Craigievar
the summer nichts are lang
and lovers young gang wanderin'
the birken groves amang
Autumn comes tae Craigievar
tae goud the geans wi' flame
and gloamin' mist brings quaitness
tae Craigievar ma hame
E'en winter deep in Craigievar
Is nae sae hard tae thole
As is the dreary loneliness
This toon brings tae my soul
But spring brings joy tae Craigievar
That rugs the hert wi' pain
For a' the howe is verdant syne
And bird sang fills the glen

Came November and squibs. Firework parties and displays were not on Scottish kids' agendas and consequently we devised our own celebration of the event which almost blew Jamie the Saxth aff his throne. One dark evening three 'French Resistance fighters' crouched in a ditch alongside the road bordering the

Pleasure Park, waiting for a German armoured car to come along. Clutched in each of their fists was a 'Little Demon' with enough explosive to blow the hated Boche to kingdom come. And sure enough, the unsuspecting enemy appeared, the bangers were lit and with superb timing, tossed underneath the vehicle where they exploded with magnificent effect. But far from a triumphant scene of flaming wreckage and soldier carnage, an emergency stop brought the car to a screeching halt and the occupant leapt out, intent on inflicting his own carnage on the by now terrified perpetrators.

Leaping out of their hiding place, the three ran like they'd never run before, pursued across the Park by their erstwhile victim whose stream of oaths left them in no doubt of the fate that awaited them. The chiel was clearly out for blood and gaining fast and it was only when the three loons instinctively split and went off in different directions that his momentary confusion gave them the chance to escape into the darkness, eventually throwing themselves down with bursting lungs and racing hearts in their separate hiding places.

Now winter had indeed arrived with its downed power lines, closed branch lines and stranded trains, as Arctic north easterlies swept snowstorms across the region, defeating all the efforts of snow ploughs to battle their way through mountainous drifts. This gave rise to the herculean efforts of local volunteers who broke out of their snow fastnesses, arriving in gangs to dig out the snowbound trains buried in railway cuttings carved out by railway navvies a century before.

Such a situation occurred between Tillyfourie and Whitehouse when a gang of volunteers was transported by train from Alford to a blocked cutting. Piling out of the carriage they got to work with shovels and sweat while one of their number, Speedy Mitchell of charcoal biscuit fame, decided to remain in the relative comfort and work free zone of the carriage. Shortly afterwards, Speedy noted that the carriage was running backwards and gaining speed on the downward slope towards Alford. It had in fact been detached to allow the engine to support snow clearance with its plough. Now brakeless and released from its heavier companion, it was free to return to base on its own volition.

Speedy by name and speedy by nature, our hero swiftly calculated his options – to leap into the comparative safety of the deep track-side wreaths or wind up pulverised as the errant carriage smashed into the buffers at Alford. Selecting the first option, he landed shocked but uninjured in the snow while the carriage glided to a gentle halt a few hundred yards beyond Whitehouse. The spot thereafter became known as 'Speedy's Loup'.

Soon the sub zero temperatures had frozen solid the flooded curling and skating ponds deep in Haughton woods, repaying the efforts of curlers and skaters who had cleared the beds of rushes during the autumn. And when the sport got underway on a freezing night, the unsuspecting traveller treading through the crisp snow could well have imagined himself in Tam o' Shanter country,

'When, glimmering thro' the groaning trees,
Kirk-Alloway seem'd in a bleeze
Through ilka bore the beams were glancing,
And loud resounded mirth and dancing'

Train stuck in snow

... as indeed the lightbulbs of the 'curler' and the Tilley lamps of the 'skater' created a magical background of illuminations and fitful shadows to accompany the shouts and laughter, scraping of skates and roaring of curling stones.

While the curlers launched their polished granite stones across the 'curler', so the skaters launched themselves across the 'skater', wielding 'sticks' cut from the branches of the surrounding trees and trimmed to perfection. Thus equipped they were ready for the night's ice hockey, all comers, no holds barred encounters, wearing ancient skates handed down within families until they ended up at some roup where they were eagerly seized upon by the village loons. The intensity of these games was such that on the coldest of nights the players were perspiring freely within minutes of action, while their smoking breath betrayed the bitter temperatures.

The mention of smoking recalls the compelling image of Rev Begg's eldest son John (yes, he of the goalmouth incident) who, despite his strict manse upbringing, introduced our little circle to the sophisticated pleasures of nicotine. One night, as we hurtled around the pond, smashing the puck in all directions, colliding with each other and falling over more frequently than staying on our skates, we became aware of a body skidding across the ice with flames and smoke billowing from its rear like a downed Messerschmitt in the Battle of Britain. It was John, whose Swan Vestas had ignited in the back pocket of his breeks through the friction caused by his skidding backside making prolonged contact with the ice.

At Christmas, the village hall once more came into its own when a party was held for the local children and 'Sunty', alias Pa Gray, arrived in suitably dramatic style. The unexpected sound of a helicopter overhead gradually silenced the young partygoers until there was hardly a movement in the hall. At that point a hatch just below the ceiling flew open and there, beaming down on the cheering assemblage, was Pa who made his precipitous way down a stairway to the floor where he was mobbed.

A few yards up the road from the village hall stood the drill hall where, as its name suggestz, more serious matters took place, in short, the defence of Her Majesty's realm. Here we were initiated into the Army Cadet Force by Sergeant Charlie Monk, given real uniforms and taught to fire live 303 rounds in the

The Vale of Alford Curling Club

adjoining rifle range – Lads' Army had arrived.

And now Christmas was here and with it the annual Cadet Christmas Ball and the chance to strut our stuff before the adoring gaze of those partners fortunate enough to receive invitations from the fledgling Gordons. Strangely, when through blin' drift we manfully escorted our partners who were sensibly encased in winter headgear, coats and wellies, then beheld their cloakroom transformation into crinoline dresses, high heels and bouffant hairstyles, the confidence inspired by khaki tunics, breeks and a jaunty heilan' bonnet thawed perceptibly.

And as surely as night follows day and the seasons come and

go, so Hogmanay arrived with its eagerly anticipated first foots clutching their lumps of coal and bottles of whisky to wish A Guid New Year tae ane an' a' and opine that 'lang may their lums reek wi' ither folks' coal'.

Epilogue

L ooking back, the post war years of the 1950s – with the advent of television and the consequent explosion of consumerism – must have accelerated the decline of village communities and in this Alford was no different. Indeed, during the late 60s, now married and returned from abroad, I came back to the village only to find a drab and deserted Main Street. A couple of years later however, an inspired Aberdeen County Council instigated a project from which, phoenix like, Haughton estate symbolically rose from the splintered timbers of the Tarzan tree.

In his article for *The Press & Journal* in September 1972, Cuthbert Graham wrote:

❝Now as the result of an imaginative scheme which won the blessing and support of the Countryside Commission, Haughton House and its policies is being converted into a delightful visitor centre which will be developed in a series of phases…

Alford is no longer a 'railway town', but in all the changes of the present century it has continued to prosper and grow while the folk in its country hinterland dwindled. It is a bulwark against the tendency

Alford's Haughton House magnet

By Cuthbert Graham

A Hairst Tae Min' On

to divide the land into big cities and depopulated rural areas, for it offers a 'third choice' – a country service centre which is big enough to sustain its own Academy and act as the hub of a viable sub-region of redoubtable character.

In the age of the motor car it is far from remote: 'just half an hour from Dyce Airport' and therefore an attractive residential village. The acquisition and development of Haughton House will bring it new visitors and admirers and the growth of Alford Academy will keep it in the forefront of educational advance. "

I am happy to say that what Graham forecast 40 years ago has indeed come to pass. Alford is a vibrant community with an expanding commuter population, still far enough away from Aberdeen to retain its unique identity. Perhaps the nostalgic amongst us might feel that the new incomers and housing developments threaten the character of the village of our youth. For my part, however, Alford is responding to the inevitable challenges of change around us and will continues to preserve, at least in my lifetime, a village and an age when it was good to be alive.